T0274197

Introduction to
Software Engineering

Introduction to Software Engineering

Theodore Hammond

 Larsen & Keller
www.larsen-keller.com

Introduction to Software Engineering
Theodore Hammond
ISBN: 978-1-64172-639-9 (Hardback)

 Larsen & Keller

Published by Larsen and Keller Education,
5 Penn Plaza,
19th Floor,
New York, NY 10001, USA

Cataloging-in-Publication Data

Introduction to software engineering / Theodore Hammond.
    p. cm.
Includes bibliographical references and index.
ISBN 978-1-64172-639-9
1. Software engineering. 2. Computer software. I. Hammond, Theodore.
QA76.758 .I58 2022
005.1--dc23

For more information regarding Larsen and Keller Education and its products, please visit the publisher's website www.larsen-keller.com

Table of Contents

Preface

The systematic application of engineering to develop software is known as software engineering. It includes designing, implementing, documenting and testing the software. There are numerous sub-disciplines within this field such as software design, software construction and software maintenance. Software designing is the process wherein the components, interfaces and other characteristics of a system are defined. The use of programming, verification, integration testing and a few other processes to create a meaningful and functioning software is known as software construction. Providing cost effective support to software through various activities is known as software maintenance. This book provides significant information of this discipline to help develop a good understanding of software engineering and related fields. Some of the diverse topics covered in this book address the varied branches that fall under this category. This book will prove to be immensely beneficial to students and researchers associated with software engineering.

A foreword of all Chapters of the book is provided below:

Chapter 1 - The branch of engineering which seeks to apply scientific and technical knowledge in order to design, test and implement software is known as software engineering. The topics elaborated in this chapter will help in gaining a better perspective about software engineering and its challenges as well as the components of a computer.; **Chapter 2** - There are a number of different methodologies which are used within software engineering to develop software such as agile methodologies, waterfall method, spiral model and incremental iteration model. These methodologies and their diverse applications have been thoroughly discussed in this chapter.; **Chapter 3** - The study which evaluates the practicality and viability of the software solution that is being considered to fulfill the requirements is known as a feasibility study. The topics elaborated in this chapter will help in gaining a better perspective about different facets which are examined in feasibility studies such as economic and technical feasibility.; **Chapter 4** - The document which details what the software will do and how is it expected to perform is known as software requirements specification. Some of the types of software requirements are functional and non-functional requirements. The chapter closely examines these key types of software requirements to provide an extensive understanding of the subject.; **Chapter 5** - The domain of computer science which deals with the creation of the fundamental structures of a software system is known as software architecture. This chapter has been carefully written to provide an easy understanding of the varied facets of computer architecture as well as the different types of architectural design patterns.; **Chapter 6** - The process which is involved in envisioning and defining software solutions to one or more sets of problems is referred to as software design. The patterns which are used to describe solutions to common problems are known as design patterns. The diverse aspects of software design as well as the different types of design patterns have been thoroughly discussed in this chapter.; **Chapter 7** - The design of different types of software interfaces which enable the users to interact with the computers is software user interface design. Graphical user interface is a common type of user interface. The chapter closely examines the key concepts of software user interface design and construction to provide an extensive understanding of the subject.; **Chapter 8** - The investigation which is conducted for providing stakeholders with information about the quality of a software product or service is known software testing. The different types of software testing are primarily divided into functional testing and non-functional testing. This chapter discusses in detail the different types of software testing as well as levels of software testing.; **Chapter 9** - The modification of a software product after delivery in order to correct the faults and to improve performance or other attributes is called software maintenance. The topics elaborated in this chapter will help in gaining a better perspective about the software maintenance process as well as the types of software maintenance.

I would like to thank the entire editorial team who made sincere efforts for this book and my family who supported me in my efforts of working on this book. I take this opportunity to thank all those who have been a guiding force throughout my life.

Theodore Hammond

Understanding Software Engineering

The branch of engineering which seeks to apply scientific and technical knowledge in order to design, test and implement software is known as software engineering. The topics elaborated in this chapter will help in gaining a better perspective about software engineering and its challenges as well as the components of a computer.

The term software engineering is the product of two words, software, and engineering. The software is a collection of integrated programs. Software subsists of carefully-organized instructions and code written by developers on any of various particular computer languages.

Computer programs and related documentation such as requirements, design models and user manuals.

Engineering is the application of scientific and practical knowledge to invent, design, build, maintain, and improve frameworks, processes, etc.

Software Engineering is an engineering branch related to the evolution of software product using well-defined scientific principles, techniques, and procedures. The result of software engineering is an effective and reliable software product.

Software Engineering is required due to the following reasons:

- To manage Large software,

- For more Scalability,

- Cost Management,

- To manage the dynamic nature of software,

- For better quality Management.

Need of Software Engineering

The necessity of software engineering appears because of a higher rate of progress in user requirements and the environment on which the program is working.

- Huge Programming: It is simpler to manufacture a wall than to a house or building, similarly, as the measure of programming become extensive engineering has to step to give it a scientific process.

- Adaptability: If the software procedure were not based on scientific and engineering ideas, it would be simpler to re-create new software than to scale an existing one.

- **Cost:** As the hardware industry has demonstrated its skills and huge manufacturing has let down the cost of computer and electronic hardware. But the cost of programming remains high if the proper process is not adapted.

- **Dynamic Nature:** The continually growing and adapting nature of programming hugely depends upon the environment in which the client works. If the quality of the software is continually changing, new upgrades need to be done in the existing one.

- **Quality Management:** Better procedure of software development provides a better and quality software product.

Challenges in Software Engineering

Software engineering employs a well-defined and systematic approach to develop software. This approach is considered to be the most effective way of producing high-quality software. However, despite this systematic approach in software development, there are still some serious challenges faced by software engineering. Some of these challenges are listed below:

- The methods used to develop small or medium-scale projects are not suitable when it comes to the development of large-scale or complex systems.

- Changes in software development are unavoidable. In today's world, changes occur rapidly and accommodating these changes to develop complete software is one of the major challenges faced by the software engineers.

- The advancement in computer and software technology has necessitated for the changes in nature of software systems. The software systems that cannot accommodate changes are not of much use. Thus, one of the challenges of software engineering is to produce high quality software adapting to the changing needs within acceptable schedules. To meet this challenge, the object oriented approach is preferred, but accommodating changes to software and its maintenance within acceptable cost is still a challenge.

- Informal communications take up a considerable portion of the time spent on software projects. Such wastage of time delays the completion of projects in the specified time.

- The user generally has only a vague idea about the scope and requirements of the software system. This usually results in the development of software, which does not meet the user's requirements.

- Changes are usually incorporated in documents without following any standard procedure. Thus, verification of all such changes often becomes difficult.

- The development of high-quality and reliable software requires the software to be thoroughly tested. Though thorough testing of software consumes the majority of resources, underestimating it because of any reasons deteriorates the software quality.

In addition to the above mentioned key challenges, the responsibilities of the system analyst, designers, and programmers are usually not well defined. Also, if the user requirements are not precisely defined, software developers can misinterpret the meaning. All these challenges need to be addressed in order to ensure that the software is developed within the specified time and estimated costs and also meets the requirements specified by the user.

Component of a Computer

A computer system consists of both hardware and information stored on hardware. Information stored on computer hardware is often called software.

- The hardware components of a computer system are the electronic and mechanical parts.

- The software components of a computer system are the data and the computer programs.

The major hardware components of a computer system are:

- Processor
- Main memory
- Secondary memory
- Input devices
- Output devices

For typical desktop computers, the processor, main memory, secondary memory, power supply, and supporting hardware are housed in a metal case. Many of the components are connected to the main circuit board of the computer, called the motherboard. The power supply supplies power for most of the components. Various input devices (such as the keyboard) and output devices (such as the monitor) are attached through connectors at the rear of the case.

The terms input and output say if data flow into or out of the computer. The picture shows the major hardware components of a computer system. The arrows show the direction of data flow.

A bus is a group of wires on the main circuit board of the computer. It is a pathway for data flowing between components. Most devices are connected to the bus through a controller which coordinates the activities of the device with the bus.

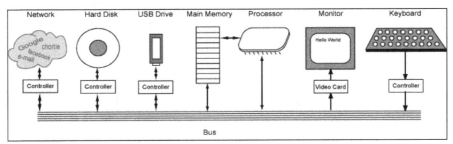

Main Components of a Computer System.

The processor is an electronic device about a one inch square, covered in plastic. Inside the square is an even smaller square of silicon containing millions of tiny electrical parts. A modern processor may contain billions of transistors. It does the fundamental computing within the system, and directly or indirectly controls all the other components.

The processor is sometimes called the Central Processing Unit or CPU. A particular computer will have a particular type of processor, such as a Pentium processor or a SPARC processor.

Project Management

Project Management is the application of knowledge, skills, tools and techniques to project activities to meet the project requirements.

Project management process consists of the following 4 stages:

- Feasibility study
- Project Planning
- Project Execution
- Project Termination

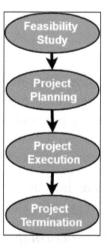

Feasibility Study

Feasibility study explores system requirements to determine project feasibility. There are several fields of feasibility study including economic feasibility, operational feasibility, and technical feasibility. The goal is to determine whether the system can be implemented or not. The process of feasibility study takes as input the requirement details as specified by the user and other domain-specific details. The output of this process simply tells whether the project should be undertaken or not and if yes, what would the constraints be. Additionally, all the risks and their potential effects on the projects are also evaluated before a decision to start the project is taken.

Project Planning

A detailed plan stating stepwise strategy to achieve the listed objectives is an integral part of any project.

Planning consists of the following activities:

- Set objectives or goals,
- Develop strategies,
- Develop project policies,
- Determine courses of action,
- Making planning decisions,
- Set procedures and rules for the project,
- Develop a software project plan,
- Prepare budget,
- Conduct risk management,
- Document software project plans.

This step also involves the construction of a work breakdown structure (WBS). It also includes size, effort, schedule and cost estimation using various techniques.

Project Execution

A project is executed by choosing an appropriate software development lifecycle model (SDLC). It includes a number of steps including requirements analysis, design, coding, testing and implementation, testing, delivery and maintenance. There are a number of factors that need to be considered while doing so including the size of the system, the nature of the project, time and budget constraints, domain requirements, etc. An inappropriate SDLC can lead to failure of the project.

Project Termination

There can be several reasons for the termination of a project. Though expecting a project to terminate after successful completion is conventional, but at times, a project may also terminate without completion. Projects have to be closed down when the requirements are not fulfilled according to given time and cost constraints.

Some of the reasons for failure include:

- Fast changing technology,
- Project running out of time,
- Organizational politics,
- Too much change in customer requirements,
- Project exceeding budget or funds.

Once the project is terminated, a post-performance analysis is done. Also, a final report is published describing the experiences, lessons learned, recommendations for handling future projects.

2

Software Engineering Methodologies

There are a number of different methodologies which are used within software engineering to develop software such as agile methodologies, waterfall method, spiral model and incremental iteration model. These methodologies and their diverse applications have been thoroughly discussed in this chapter.

Development methodologies are a battle between dogmatism and pragmatism. Dogmatism is people who just have zeal – they say that this way is the way, if you deviate from this way, all is lost. Pragmatism, pulling together what works in the moment.

There are definite benefits to both. The people who are more dogmatic versus pragmatic, produce a better level of insight into the system; because they're really spending a lot of time focusing on their tool and what it can do and how to optimise it. They produce a better raw product. Pragmatists can look at all of these raw products and say, that this bit can be taken from there and that bit from there and can be more effective when it comes to changing requirements and changing projects.

Software development methodology is a process or series of processes used in software development. Again, quite broad but that it is things like a design phase, a development phase. It is ways of thinking about things like waterfall being a non iterative kind of process. Generally it takes the form of defined phases. It is designed to describe the how of the life cycle of a piece of software.

Surely there couldn't be that many different software development methodologies. There are as many as you can possibly find and pretty much any time someone has one and decides to vary it even slightly from an existing one, they will put a new label on it and call it something new. That makes it quite hard to be across all of the different types.

Waterfall

Waterfall model is an example of a Sequential model. In this model, the software development activity is divided into different phases and each phase consists of series of tasks and has different objectives.

Waterfall model is the pioneer of the SDLC processes. In fact, it was the first model which was widely used in the software industry. It is divided into phases and output of one phase becomes the input of the next phase. It is mandatory for a phase to be completed before the next phase starts. In short, there is no overlapping in Waterfall model.

In waterfall, development of one phase starts only when the previous phase is complete. Because of this nature, each phase of waterfall model is quite precise well defined. Since the phases fall from higher level to lower level, like a waterfall, it's named as waterfall model.

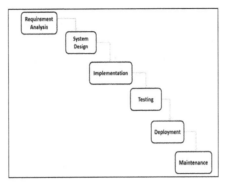

Pictorial representation of waterfall model.

The activities involved in different phases are as follows:

S. No	Phase	Activities Performed	Deliverables
1	Requirement Analysis	1. Capture all the requirements. 2. Do brainstorming and walkthrough to understand the requirements. 3. Do the requirements feasibility test to ensure that the requirements are testable or not.	RUD (Requirements Understanding Document)
2	System Design	1. As per the requirements, create the design. 2. Capture the hardware / software requirements. 3. Document the designs.	HLD (High Level Design document) LLD (Low level design document)
3	Implementation	1. As per the design create the programmes / code. 2. Integrate the codes for the next phase. 3. Unit testing of the code.	Programs Unit test cases and results
4	System Testing	1. Integrate the unit tested code and test it to make sure if it works as expected. 2. Perform all the testing activities (Functional and non-functional) to make sure that the system meets the requirements. 3. In case of any anomaly, report it. 4. Track your progress on testing through tools like traceability metrics, ALM. 5. Report your testing activities.	Test cases Test reports Defect reports Updated matrices.
5	System Deployment	1. Make sure that the environment is up 2. Make sure that there are no sev 1 defects open. 3. Make sure that the test exit criteria are met. 4. Deploy the application in the respective environment. 5. Perform a sanity check in the environment after the application is deployed to ensure the application does not break.	User Manual Environment definition / specification

6	System maintenance	1. Make sure that the application is up and running in the respective environment.	User Manual
		2. In case user encounters and defect, make sure to note and fix the issues faced.	List of production tickets
		3. In case any issue is fixed; the updated code is deployed in the environment.	List of new features implemented.
		4. The application is always enhanced to incorporate more features, update the environment with the latest features.	

When to use SDLC Waterfall Model?

SDLC Waterfall model is used when:

- Requirements are stable and not changed frequently.
- An application is small.
- There is no requirement which is not understood or not very clear.
- The environment is stable.
- The tools and technology used is stable and is not dynamic.
- Resources are well trained and are available.

Pros and Cons of Waterfall Model

Advantages of using Waterfall model are as follows:

- Simple and easy to understand and use.
- For smaller projects, waterfall model works well and yield the appropriate results.
- Since the phases are rigid and precise, one phase is done one at a time, it is easy to maintain.
- The entry and exit criteria are well defined, so it easy and systematic to proceed with quality.
- Results are well documented.

Disadvantages of using Waterfall model:

- Cannot adopt the changes in requirements.
- It becomes very difficult to move back to the phase. For example, if the application has now moved to the testing stage and there is a change in requirement, It becomes difficult to go back and change it.
- Delivery of the final product is late as there is no prototype which is demonstrated intermediately.
- For bigger and complex projects, this model is not good as a risk factor is higher.
- Not suitable for the projects where requirements are changed frequently.

- Does not work for long and on-going projects.

- Since the testing is done at a later stage, it does not allow identifying the challenges and risks in the earlier phase so the risk mitigation strategy is difficult to prepare.

Agile Methodologies

Agile software development is more than frameworks such as Scrum, Extreme Programming or Feature-Driven Development (FDD). It is more than practices such as pair programming, test-driven development, stand-ups, planning sessions and sprints. It is an umbrella term for a set of frameworks and practices based on the values and principles expressed in the Manifesto for Agile Software Development and the 12 Principles behind it. When you approach software development in a particular manner, it's generally good to live by these values and principles and use them to help figure out the right things to do given your particular context.

One thing that separates Agile from other approaches to software development is the focus on the people doing the work and how they work together. Solutions evolve through collaboration between self-organizing cross-functional teams utilizing the appropriate practices for their context.

There's a big focus in the agile software development community on collaboration and the self-organizing team.

That doesn't mean that there aren't managers. It means that teams have the ability to figure out how they're going to approach things on their own.

It means that those teams are cross-functional. Those teams don't have to have specific roles involved so much as that when you get the team together, you make sure that you have all the right skill sets on the team.

There still is a place for managers. Managers make sure team members have, or obtain, the right skill sets. Managers provide the environment that allows the team to be successful. Managers mostly step back and let their team figure out how they are going to deliver products, but they step in when the teams try but are unable to resolve issues.

When most teams and organizations start doing agile software development, they focus on the practices that help with collaboration and organizing the work, which is great. However, another key set of practices that are not as frequently followed but should be are specific technical practices that directly deal with developing software. An agile software development process always starts by defining the users and documenting a vision statement on a scope of problems, opportunities, and values to be addressed. The product owner captures this vision and works with a multidisciplinary team (or teams) to deliver on this vision. Here are the roles in that process.

User

Agile processes always begin with the user or customer in mind. Today, we often define them with user personas to illustrate different roles in a workflow the software is supporting or different types of customer needs and behaviors.

Product Owner

The agile development process itself begins with someone who is required to be the voice of the customer, including any internal stakeholders. That person distills all the insights, ideas, and feedback to create a product vision. These visions are often simple and short, but they nonetheless paint a picture of who the customer is, what values are being addressed, and a strategy on how to address them. You can imagine Google's original vision looked something like "Let's make it easy for anyone with internet access to find relevant websites and webpages with a simple, keyword-driven interface and an algorithm that ranks reputable sources higher in the search results."

We call this this person the *product owner*. His or her responsibility is to define this vision and then work with a development team to make it real.

To work with the development team, the product owner breaks down the vision to a series of user stories that spell out more detail on who the target user is what problem is being solved for them, why it's important for them, and what constraints and acceptance criteria define the solution. These user stories are prioritized by the product owner, reviewed by the team to ensure they have a shared understanding on what is being asked of them.

Software Development Team

In agile, the development team and its members' responsibilities differ from those in traditional software development.

Teams are multidisciplinary, composed of a diverse group of people with the skills to get the job done. Because the focus is on delivering working software, the team has to complete end-to-end functioning applications. So the database, business logic, and user interface of *part* of the application is developed and then demoed—not the whole application. To do this, the team members have to collaborate on what and how they are developing. To do that, they meet frequently to make sure everyone is aligned on who is doing what, and how the software is actually being developed.

In addition to developers, software development teams can include quality assurance (QA) engineers, other engineers (such as for databases and back-end systems), designers, and analysts, depending on the type of software project.

Benefits of Agile Methodology

The benefits of Agile are tied directly to its faster, lighter, more engaged mind-set. The process, in a nutshell, delivers what the customer wants, when the customer wants it. There's much less wasted time spent developing in the wrong direction, and the entire system is quicker to respond to changes.

- Faster: Speed is one of the biggest benefits of Agile Methodology. A faster software development life cycle means less time between paying and getting paid. That, in turn, means a more profitable business.

- Increased customer satisfaction: With Agile, customers don't wait for months or years, only to get exactly what they didn't want. Instead, they get iterations of something very close to what they want, very fast. The system adjusts quickly to refine the successful customer solution, adapting as it goes to changes in the overall environment.

- Values employees: Employees whose ideas are valued are vastly more productive than those who are ordered to follow a set of rules. The Agile Methodology respects employees by giving them the goal, then trusting them to reach it. Since they're the ones with their hands on the controls and the ones who see the obstacles that crop up every day, employees are in the best position to respond to challenges and meet the goals at hand.

- Eliminates rework: By involving the customer at more than just the phases of requirements and delivery, the project remains on-task and in-tune with customer needs at every step. This means less backtracking and less "out on a limb" time between the time we do the work and the time the customer suggests revisions.

Agile vs. Waterfall Method

Agile and Waterfall model are two different methods for software development process. Though they are different in their approach, both methods are useful at times, depending on the requirement and the type of the project.

Agile Model	Waterfall Model
• Agile method proposes incremental and iterative approach to software design.	• Development of the software flows sequentially from start point to end point.
• The agile process is broken into individual models that designers work on.	• The design process is not broken into an individual models.
• The customer has early and frequent opportunities to look at the product and make decision and changes to the project.	• The customer can only see the product at the end of the project.
• Agile model is considered unstructured compared to the waterfall model.	• Waterfall model are more secure because they are so plan oriented.
• Small projects can be implemented very quickly. For large projects, it is difficult to estimate the development time.	• All sorts of project can be estimated and completed.
• Error can be fixed in the middle of the project.	• Only at the end, the whole product is tested. If the requirement error is found or any changes have to be made, the project has to start from the beginning.
• Development process is iterative, and the project is executed in short (2-4) weeks iterations. Planning is very less.	• The development process is phased, and the phase is much bigger than iteration. Every phase ends with the detailed description of the next phase.
• Documentation attends less priority than software development.	• Documentation is a top priority and can even use for training staff and upgrade the software with another team.
• Every iteration has its own testing phase. It allows implementing regression testing every time new functions or logic are released.	• Only after the development phase, the testing phase is executed because separate parts are not fully functional.

• In agile testing when an iteration end, shippable features of the product is delivered to the customer. New features are usable right after shipment. It is useful when you have good contact with customers.	• All features developed are delivered at once after the long implementation phase.
• Testers and developers work together.	• Testers work separately from developers.
• At the end of every sprint, user acceptance is performed.	• User acceptance is performed at the end of the project.
• It requires close communication with developers and together analyze requirements and planning.	• Developer does not involve in requirement and planning process. Usually, time delays between tests and coding.

Rational Unified Process

The Rational Unified Process is a Software Engineering Process. It provides a disciplined approach to assigning tasks and responsibilities within a development organization. Its goal is to ensure the production of high-quality software that meets the needs of its end-users, within a predictable schedule and budget.

It is a process product, developed and maintained by Rational Software. The development teams for the Rational Unified Process are working closely with customers, partners, Rational's product groups as well as Rational's consultant organization, to ensure that the process is continuously updated and improved upon to reflect recent experiences and evolving and proven best practices.

It enhances team productivity, by providing every team member with easy access to a knowledge base with guidelines, templates and tool mentors for all critical development activities. By having all team members accessing the same knowledge base, no matter if you work with requirements, design, test, project management, or configuration management, we ensure that all team members share a common language, process and view of how to develop software.

It activities create and maintain models. Rather than focusing on the production of large amount of paper documents, the Unified Process emphasizes the development and maintenance of models—semantically rich representations of the software system under development.

The Rational Unified Process is a guide for how to effectively use the Unified Modeling Language (UML). The UML is an industry-standard language that allows us to clearly communicate requirements, architectures and designs. The UML was originally created by Rational Software, and is now maintained by the standards organization Object Management Group (OMG).

The Rational Unified Process is supported by tools, which automate large parts of the process. They are used to create and maintain the various artifacts—models in particular—of the software engineering process: visual modeling, programming, testing, etc. They are invaluable in supporting all the bookkeeping associated with the change management as well as the configuration management that accompanies each iteration.

The Rational Unified Process is a configurable process. No single process is suitable for all software development. The Unified Process fits small development teams as well as large development organizations. The Unified Process is founded on a simple and clear process architecture that provides commonality across a family of processes. Yet, it can be varied to accommodate different situations. It contains a Development Kit, providing support for configuring the process to suit the needs of a given organization.

The Rational Unified Process captures many of the best practices in modern software development in a form that is suitable for a wide range of projects and organizations. Deploying these best practices using the Rational Unified Process as your guide offers development teams a number of key advantages. In next section, we describe the six fundamental best practices of the Rational Unified Process.

Effective Deployment of 6 Best Practices

The Rational Unified Process describes how to effectively deploy commercially proven approaches to software development for software development teams. These are called "best practices" not so much because you can precisely quantify their value, but rather, because they are observed to be commonly used in industry by successful organizations. The Rational Unified Process provides each team member with the guidelines, templates and tool mentors necessary for the entire team to take full advantage of among others the following best practices:

- Develop software iteratively.

- Manage requirements.

- Use component-based architectures.

- Visually model software.

- Verify software quality.

- Control changes to software.

Develop Software Iteratively

Given today's sophisticated software systems, it is not possible to sequentially first define the entire problem, design the entire solution, build the software and then test the product at the end. An iterative approach is required that allows an increasing understanding of the problem through successive refinements, and to incrementally grow an effective solution over multiple iterations. The Rational Unified Process supports an iterative approach to development that addresses the highest risk items at every stage in the lifecycle, significantly reducing a project's risk profile. This iterative approach helps you attack risk through demonstrable progress frequent, executable releases that enable continuous end user involvement and feedback. Because each iteration ends with an executable release, the development team stays focused on producing results, and frequent status checks help ensure that the project stays on schedule. An iterative approach also makes it easier to accommodate tactical changes in requirements, features or schedule.

Manage Requirements

The Rational Unified Process describes how to elicit, organize, and document required functionality and constraints; track and document tradeoffs and decisions; and easily capture and communicate business requirements. The notions of use case and scenarios proscribed in the process has proven to be an excellent way to capture functional requirements and to ensure that these drive the design, implementation and testing of software, making it more likely that the final system fulfills the end user needs. They provide coherent and traceable threads through both the development and the delivered system.

Use Component-based Architectures

The process focuses on early development and base lining of a robust executable architecture, prior to committing resources for full-scale development. It describes how to design a resilient architecture that is flexible, accommodates change, is intuitively understandable, and promotes more effective software reuse. The Rational Unified Process supports component-based software development.

Components are non-trivial modules, subsystems that fulfill a clear function. The Rational Unified Process provides a systematic approach to defining an architecture using new and existing components. These are assembled in a well-defined architecture, either ad hoc, or in a component infrastructure such as the Internet, CORBA, and COM, for which an industry of reusable components is emerging.

Visually Model Software

The process shows you how to visually model software to capture the structure and behavior of architectures and components. This allows you to hide the details and write code using "graphical building blocks." Visual abstractions help you communicate different aspects of your software; see how the elements of the system fit together; make sure that the building blocks are consistent with your code; maintain consistency between a design and its implementation; and promote unambiguous communication. The industry- standard Unified Modeling Language (UML), created by Rational Software, is the foundation for successful visual modeling.

Verify Software Quality

Poor application performance and poor reliability are common factors which dramatically inhibit the acceptability of today's software applications. Hence, quality should be reviewed with respect to the requirements based on reliability, functionality, application performance and system performance. The Rational Unified Process assists you in the planning, design, implementation, execution, and evaluation of these test types. Quality assessment is built into the process, in all activities, involving all participants, using objective measurements and criteria, and not treated as an afterthought or a separate activity performed by a separate group.

Control Changes to Software

The ability to manage change is making certain that each change is acceptable, and being able to track changes is essential in an environment in which change is inevitable. The process describes how to control, track and monitor changes to enable successful iterative development. It also guides you in how to establish secure workspaces for each developer by providing isolation from changes made in other workspaces and by controlling changes of all software artifacts (e.g., models, code, documents, etc.). And it brings a team together to work as a single unit by describing how to automate integration and build management.

Process

Two Dimensions

The process can be described in two dimensions, or along two axis:

- The horizontal axis represents time and shows the dynamic aspect of the process as it is enacted, and it is expressed in terms of cycles, phases, iterations, and milestones.

- The vertical axis represents the static aspect of the process: how it is described in terms of activities, artifacts, workers and workflows.

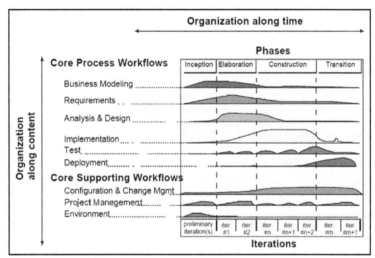

The Iterative Model graph shows how the process is structured along two dimensions.

Phases and Iterations - The Time Dimension

This is the dynamic organization of the process along time.

The software lifecycle is broken into cycles, each cycle working on a new generation of the product. The Rational Unified Process divides one development cycle in four consecutive *phases:*

- Inception phase
- Elaboration phase
- Construction phase
- Transition phase

Each phase is concluded with a well-defined milestone—a point in time at which certain critical decisions must be made and therefore key goals must have been achieved.

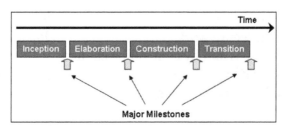

The phases and major milestones in the process.

Each phase has a specific purpose.

Inception Phase

During the inception phase, you establish the business case for the system and delimit the project scope. To accomplish this you must identify all external entities with which the system will interact (actors) and define the nature of this interaction at a high-level. This involves identifying all use cases and describing a few significant ones. The business case includes success criteria, risk assessment, and estimate of the resources needed, and a phase plan showing dates of major milestones. The outcome of the inception phase is:

- A vision document: a general vision of the core project's requirements, key features, and main constraints.

- A initial use-case model (10% -20%) complete).

- An initial project glossary (may optionally be partially expressed as a domain model).

- An initial business case, which includes business context, success criteria (revenue projection, market recognition, and so on), and financial forecast.

- An initial risk assessment.

- A project plan, showing phases and iterations.

- A business model, if necessary.

- One or several prototypes.

Milestone: Lifecycle Objectives

At the end of the inception phase is the first major project milestone: the Lifecycle Objectives Milestone. The evaluation criteria for the inception phase are:

- Stakeholder concurrence on scope definition and cost/schedule estimates.

- Requirements understanding as evidenced by the fidelity of the primary use cases.

- Credibility of the cost/schedule estimates, priorities, risks, and development process.

- Depth and breadth of any architectural prototype that was developed.

- Actual expenditures versus planned expenditures.

The project may be cancelled or considerably re-thought if it fails to pass this milestone.

Elaboration Phase

The purpose of the elaboration phase is to analyze the problem domain, establish a sound architectural foundation, develop the project plan, and eliminate the highest risk elements of the project. To accomplish these objectives, you must have the "mile wide and inch deep" view of the system. Architectural decisions have to be made with an understanding of the whole system: its scope, major functionality and nonfunctional requirements such as performance requirements.

It is easy to argue that the elaboration phase is the most critical of the four phases. At the end of this phase, the hard "engineering" is considered complete and the project undergoes its most important day of reckoning: the decision on whether or not to commit to the construction and transition phases. For most projects, this also corresponds to the transition from a mobile, light and nimble, low-risk operation to a high-cost, high-risk operation with substantial inertia. While the process must always accommodate changes, the elaboration phase activities ensure that the architecture, requirements and plans are stable enough, and the risks are sufficiently mitigated, so you can predictably determine the cost and schedule for the completion of the development. Conceptually, this level of fidelity would correspond to the level necessary for an organization to commit to a fixed-price construction phase.

In the elaboration phase, an executable architecture prototype is built in one or more iterations, depending on the scope, size, risk, and novelty of the project. This effort should at least address the critical use cases identified in the inception phase, which typically expose the major technical risks of the project. While an evolutionary prototype of a production-quality component is always the goal, this does not exclude the development of one or more exploratory, throwaway prototypes to mitigate specific risks such as design/requirements trade-offs, component feasibility study, or demonstrations to investors, customers, and end-users.

The outcome of the elaboration phase is:

- A use-case model (at least 80% complete) — all use cases and actors have been identified, and most use- case descriptions have been developed.

- Supplementary requirements capturing the nonfunctional requirements and any requirements that are not associated with a specific use case.

- A Software Architecture Description.

- An executable architectural prototype.

- A revised risk list and a revised business case.

- A development plan for the overall project, including the coarse-grained project plan, showing iterations" and evaluation criteria for each iteration.

- An updated development case specifying the process to be used.

- A preliminary user manual (optional).

Milestone: Lifecycle Architecture

At the end of the elaboration phase is the second important project milestone, the Lifecycle Architecture Milestone. At this point, you examine the detailed system objectives and scope, the choice of architecture, and the resolution of the major risks.

The main evaluation criterion for the elaboration phase involves the answers to these questions:

- Is the vision of the product stable?
- Is the architecture stable?
- Does the executable demonstration show that the major risk elements have been addressed and credibly resolved?
- Is the plan for the construction phase sufficiently detailed and accurate? Is it backed up with a credible basis of estimates?
- Do all stakeholders agree that the current vision can be achieved if the current plan is executed to develop the complete system, in the context of the current architecture?
- Is the actual resource expenditure versus planned expenditure acceptable?

The project may be aborted or considerably re-thought if it fails to pass this milestone.

Construction Phase

During the construction phase, all remaining components and application features are developed and integrated into the product, and all features are thoroughly tested. The construction phase is, in one sense, a manufacturing process where emphasis is placed on managing resources and controlling operations to optimize costs, schedules, and quality. In this sense, the management mindset undergoes a transition from the development of intellectual property during inception and elaboration, to the development of deployable products during construction and transition.

Many projects are large enough that parallel construction increments can be spawned. These parallel activities can significantly accelerate the availability of deployable releases; they can also increase the complexity of resource management and workflow synchronization. A robust architecture and an understandable plan are highly correlated. In other words, one of the critical qualities of the architecture is its ease of construction. This is one reason why the balanced development of the architecture and the plan is stressed during the elaboration phase. The outcome of the construction phase is a product ready to put in hands of its end-users. At minimum, it consists of:

- The software product integrated on the adequate platforms.
- The user manuals.
- A description of the current release.

Milestone: Initial Operational Capability

At the end of the construction phase is the third major project milestone (Initial Operational Capability Milestone). At this point, you decide if the software, the sites, and the users are ready to go operational, without exposing the project to high risks. This release is often called a "beta" release.

The evaluation criteria for the construction phase involve answering these questions:

- Is this product release stable and mature enough to be deployed in the user community?

- Are all stakeholders ready for the transition into the user community?

- Are the actual resource expenditures versus planned expenditures still acceptable?

Transition may have to be postponed by one release if the project fails to reach this milestone.

Transition Phase

The purpose of the transition phase is to transition the software product to the user community. Once the product has been given to the end user, issues usually arise that require you to develop new releases, correct some problems, or finish the features that were postponed.

The transition phase is entered when a baseline is mature enough to be deployed in the end-user domain.

This typically requires that some usable subset of the system has been completed to an acceptable level of quality and that user documentation is available so that the transition to the user will provide positive results for all parties.

This includes:

- "Beta testing" to validate the new system against user expectations.

- Parallel operation with a legacy system that it is replacing.

- Conversion of operational databases.

- Training of users and maintainers.

- Roll-out the product to the marketing, distribution, and sales teams.

The transition phase focuses on the activities required to place the software into the hands of the users. Typically, this phase includes several iterations, including beta releases, general availability releases, as well as bug-fix and enhancement releases. Considerable effort is expended in developing user-oriented documentation, training users, supporting users in their initial product use, and reacting to user feedback. At this point in the lifecycle, however, user feedback should be confined primarily to product tuning, configuring, installation, and usability issues.

The primary objectives of the transition phase include:

- Achieving user self-supportability,

- Achieving stakeholder concurrence that deployment baselines are complete and consistent with the evaluation criteria of the vision,

- Achieving final product baseline as rapidly and cost effectively as practical.

This phase can range from being very simple to extremely complex, depending on the type of product. For example, a new release of an existing desktop product may be very simple, whereas replacing a nation's air-traffic control system would be very complex.

Milestone: Product Release

At the end of the transition phase is the fourth important project milestone, the Product Release Milestone. At this point, you decide if the objectives were met, and if you should start another development cycle. In some cases, this milestone may coincide with the end of the inception phase for the next cycle.

The primary evaluation criteria for the transition phase involve the answers to these questions:

- Is the user satisfied?
- Are the actual resources expenditures versus planned expenditures still acceptable?

Iterations

Each phase in the Rational Unified Process can be further broken down into iterations. Iteration is a complete development loop resulting in a release (internal or external) of an executable product, a subset of the final product under development, which grows incrementally from iteration to iteration to become the final system.

Benefits of an Iterative Approach

Compared to the traditional waterfall process, the iterative process has the following advantages:

- Risks are mitigated earlier,
- Change is more manageable,
- Higher level of reuse,
- The project team can learn along the way,
- Better overall quality.

Spiral Model

Spiral model is one of the most important Software Development Life Cycle models, which provides support for Risk Handling. In its diagrammatic representation, it looks like a spiral with many loops. The exact number of loops of the spiral is unknown and can vary from project to project. Each loop of the spiral is called a Phase of the software development process. The exact number of phases needed to develop the product can be varied by the project manager depending upon the project risks. As the project manager dynamically determines the number of phases, so the project manager has an important role to develop a product using spiral model.

The Radius of the spiral at any point represents the expenses (cost) of the project so far, and the angular dimension represents the progress made so far in the current phase.

Below diagram shows the different phases of the Spiral Model:

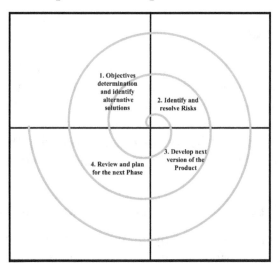

Each phase of Spiral Model is divided into four quadrants as shown in the figure. The functions of these four quadrants are discussed below:

1. Objectives determination and identify alternative solutions: Requirements are gathered from the customers and the objectives are identified, elaborated and analyzed at the start of every phase. Then alternative solutions possible for the phase are proposed in this quadrant.

2. Identify and resolve Risks: During the second quadrant all the possible solutions are evaluated to select the best possible solution. Then the risks associated with that solution is identified and the risks are resolved using the best possible strategy. At the end of this quadrant, Prototype is built for the best possible solution.

3. Develop next version of the Product: During the third quadrant, the identified features are developed and verified through testing. At the end of the third quadrant, the next version of the software is available.

4. Review and plan for the next Phase: In the fourth quadrant, the Customers evaluate the so far developed version of the software. In the end, planning for the next phase is started.

Risk Handling in Spiral Model

A risk is any adverse situation that might affect the successful completion of a software project. The most important feature of the spiral model is handling these unknown risks after the project has started. Such risk resolutions are easier done by developing a prototype. The spiral model supports coping up with risks by providing the scope to build a prototype at every phase of the software development.

Prototyping Model also support risk handling, but the risks must be identified completely before the start of the development work of the project. But in real life project risk may occur after the development work starts, in that case, we cannot use Prototyping Model. In each phase of the Spiral Model, the features of the product dated and analyzed and the risks at that point of time are identified and are resolved through prototyping. Thus, this model is much more flexible compared to other SDLC models.

Spiral Model a Meta Model

The Spiral model is called as a Meta Model because it subsumes all the other SDLC models. For example, a single loop spiral actually represents the Iterative Waterfall Model. The spiral model incorporates the stepwise approach of the Classical Waterfall Model. The spiral model uses the approach of Prototyping Model by building a prototype at the start of each phase as a risk handling technique. Also, the spiral model can be considered as supporting the evolutionary model – the iterations along the spiral can be considered as evolutionary levels through which the complete system is built.

Advantages of Spiral Model: Below are some of the advantages of the Spiral Model:

- Risk Handling: The projects with many unknown risks that occur as the development proceeds, in that case, Spiral Model is the best development model to follow due to the risk analysis and risk handling at every phase.

- Good for large projects: It is recommended to use the Spiral Model in large and complex projects.

- Flexibility in Requirements: Change requests in the Requirements at later phase can be incorporated accurately by using this model.

- Customer Satisfaction: Customer can see the development of the product at the early phase of the software development and thus, they habituated with the system by using it before completion of the total product.

Disadvantages of Spiral Model: Below are some of the main disadvantages of the spiral model:

- Complex: The Spiral Model is much more complex than other SDLC models.

- Expensive: Spiral Model is not suitable for small projects as it is expensive.

- Too much dependable on Risk Analysis: The successful completion of the project is very much dependent on Risk Analysis. Without very highly experienced expertise, it is going to be a failure to develop a project using this model.

- Difficulty in time management: As the number of phases is unknown at the start of the project, so time estimation is very difficult.

Incremental Iteration Model

In the Iterative model, iterative process starts with a simple implementation of a small set of the software requirements and iteratively enhances the evolving versions until the complete system is implemented and ready to be deployed.

An iterative life cycle model does not attempt to start with a full specification of requirements. Instead, development begins by specifying and implementing just part of the software, which is then reviewed to identify further requirements. This process is then repeated, producing a new version of the software at the end of each iteration of the model.

Iterative Model-Design

Iterative process starts with a simple implementation of a subset of the software requirements and iteratively enhances the evolving versions until the full system is implemented. At each iteration, design modifications are made and new functional capabilities are added. The basic idea behind this method is to develop a system through repeated cycles (iterative) and in smaller portions at a time (incremental).

The following illustration is a representation of the Iterative and Incremental model:

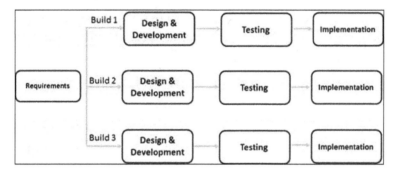

Iterative and Incremental development is a combination of both iterative design or iterative method and incremental build model for development. "During software development, more than one iteration of the software development cycle may be in progress at the same time." This process may be described as an "evolutionary acquisition" or "incremental build" approach."

In this incremental model, the whole requirement is divided into various builds. During each iteration, the development module goes through the requirements, design, implementation and testing phases. Each subsequent release of the module adds function to the previous release. The process continues till the complete system is ready as per the requirement.

The key to a successful use of an iterative software development lifecycle is rigorous validation of requirements, and verification & testing of each version of the software against those requirements within each cycle of the model. As the software evolves through successive cycles, tests must be repeated and extended to verify each version of the software.

Iterative Model-Application

Like other SDLC models, Iterative and incremental development has some specific applications in the software industry. This model is most often used in the following scenarios:

- Requirements of the complete system are clearly defined and understood.

- Major requirements must be defined; however, some functionalities or requested enhancements may evolve with time.

- There is a time to the market constraint.

- A new technology is being used and is being learnt by the development team while working on the project.

- Resources with needed skill sets are not available and are planned to be used on contract basis for specific iterations.

- There are some high-risk features and goals which may change in the future.

Iterative Model-Pros and Cons

The advantage of this model is that there is a working model of the system at a very early stage of development, which makes it easier to find functional or design flaws. Finding issues at an early stage of development enables to take corrective measures in a limited budget.

The disadvantage with this SDLC model is that it is applicable only to large and bulky software development projects. This is because it is hard to break a small software system into further small serviceable increments/modules.

The advantages of the Iterative and Incremental SDLC Model are as follows:

- Some working functionality can be developed quickly and early in the life cycle.

- Results are obtained early and periodically.

- Parallel development can be planned.

- Progress can be measured.

- Less costly to change the scope/requirements.

- Testing and debugging during smaller iteration is easy.

- Risks are identified and resolved during iteration; and each iteration is an easily managed milestone.

- Easier to manage risk - High risk part is done first.

- With every increment, operational product is delivered.

- Issues, challenges and risks identified from each increment can be utilized/applied to the next increment.

- Risk analysis is better.

- It supports changing requirements.

- Initial Operating time is less.

- Better suited for large and mission-critical projects.

- During the life cycle, software is produced early which facilitates customer evaluation and feedback.

The disadvantages of the Iterative and Incremental SDLC Model are as follows:

- More resources may be required.

- Although cost of change is lesser, but it is not very suitable for changing requirements.

- More management attention is required.

- System architecture or design issues may arise because not all requirements are gathered in the beginning of the entire life cycle.

- Defining increments may require definition of the complete system.

- Not suitable for smaller projects.

- Management complexity is more.

- End of project may not be known which is a risk.

- Highly skilled resources are required for risk analysis.

- Projects progress is highly dependent upon the risk analysis phase.

Extreme Programming

Extreme Programming (XP) is a discipline of software development based on values of simplicity, communication & feedback. It works by bringing the whole team together in the presence of simple practices, with enough feedback to enable the team to check where they are and to tune the practices to their unique situation.

XP recognizes that the end goal of a development project is to produce quality, production code that can be executed and maintained. Anything in a project that does not directly support this goal is questioned and discarded if appropriate. XP takes 12 software development "best practices," and applies them to the extreme. Every contributor to the Project is a part of the 'TEAM' and the Team interacts with the 'Customer' daily.

XP Core Practices

1. The Planning Game: Business and development cooperate to produce the maximum business value as rapidly as possible. The planning game happens at various scales, but the basic rules are the same:

- Business comes up with a list of desired features for the system. Each feature is written out as a User Story, which gives the feature a name, and describes in broad strokes what is required. User stories are typically written on 4x6 cards.

- Development estimates how much effort each story will take, and how much effort the team can produce in a given time interval.

- Business then decides which stories to implement in what order, as well as when and how often to produce a production release of the system.

2. Small Releases: XP teams practice small releases in two important ways: First, the team releases running, tested software, delivering business value chosen by the Customer, every iteration. The Customer can use this software for any purpose, whether evaluation or even release to end users. The most important aspect is that the software is visible, and given to the customer, at the end of every iteration. Second, XP teams release to their end users frequently as well. XP Web projects release as often as daily, in house projects monthly or more frequently.

3. Simple Design: XP uses the simplest possible design that gets the job done. The requirements will change tomorrow, so only do what's needed to meet today's requirements.

Design in XP is not a one-time thing but an all-the-time thing. There are design steps in release planning and iteration planning, plus teams engage in quick design sessions and design revisions through refactoring, through the course of the entire project.

4. Metaphor: Extreme Programming teams develop a common vision of how the program works, which we call the "metaphor". At its best, the metaphor is a simple evocative description of how the program works.

XP teams use a common system of names to be sure that everyone understands how the system works and where to look to find the functionality you're looking for, or to find the right place to put the functionality you're about to add.

5. Continuous Testing: XP teams focus on validation of the software at all times. Programmers develop software by writing tests first, and then code that fulfills the requirements reflected in the tests. Customers provide acceptance tests that enable them to be certain that the features they need are provided.

6. Refactoring: XP Team Refactor out any duplicate code generated in a coding session. Refactoring is simplified due to extensive use of automated test cases.

7. Pair Programming: All production code is written by two programmers sitting at one machine. This practice ensures that all code is reviewed as it is written and results in better Design, testing and better code.

Some programmers object to pair programming without ever trying it. It does take some practice to do well, and you need to do it well for a few weeks to see the results. Ninety percent of programmers who learn pair programming prefer it, so it is recommended to all teams.

Pairing, in addition to providing better code and tests, also serves to communicate knowledge throughout the team.

8. Collective Code Ownership: No single person "owns" a module. Any developer is expected to be able to work on any part of the codebase at any time.

9. Continuous Integration: All changes are integrated into the codebase at least daily. The unit tests have to run 100% both before and after integration.

Infrequent integration leads to serious problems on a software project. First of all, although integration is critical to shipping good working code, the team is not practiced at it, and often it is delegated to people who are not familiar with the whole system. Problems creep in at integration times that are not detected by any of the testing that takes place on an unintegrated system. Also weak integration process leads to long code freezes. Code freezes mean that you have long time periods when the programmers could be working on important shippable features, but that those features must be held back.

10. 40-Hour Work Week: Programmers go home on time. In crunch mode, up to one week of overtime is allowed. But multiple consecutive weeks of overtime are treated as a sign that something is very wrong with the process and/or schedule.

11. On-site Customer: Development team has continuous access to the customer who will actually be using the system. For initiatives with lots of customers, a customer representative (i.e. Product Manager) will be designated for Development team access.

12. Coding Standards: Everyone codes to the same standards. The specifics of the standard are not important: what is important is that all the he code looks familiar, in support of collective ownership.

XP Values

XP is a values-based methodology. The values are Simplicity, Communication, Feedback and Courage. XP's core values are best summarized in the following statement by Kent Beck: Do more of what works and do less of what doesn't.

Highlights of the four values are itemized below:

Simplicity encourages:

- Delivering the simplest functionality that meets business needs,
- Designing the simplest software that supports the needed functionality,
- Building for today and not for tomorrow,
- Writing code that is easy to read, understand, maintain and modify.

Communication is accomplished by:

- Collaborative workspaces,
- Co-location of development and business space,
- Paired development,
- Frequently changing pair partners,
- Frequently changing assignments,
- Public status displays,
- Short standup meetings,
- Unit tests, demos and oral communication, not documentation.

Feedback is provided by:

- Aggressive iterative and incremental releases,

- Frequent releases to end users,

- Co-location with end users,

- Automated unit tests,

- Automated functional tests,

- Courage is required to:

  ◦ Do the right thing in the face of opposition.

  ◦ Do the practices required to succeed.

SCRUM

SCRUM is a process in agile methodology which is a combination of the Iterative model and the incremental model.

One of the major handicaps of the traditional Waterfall model was that – until the first phase is complete, the application does not move to the other phase. And by chance, if there are some changes in the later stage of the cycle, then it becomes very challenging to implement those changes, as it would involve revisiting the earlier phases and redoing the changes.

Some of the key characteristics of SCRUM include:

- Self-organized and focused team.

- No huge requirement documents, rather have a very precise and to the point stories.

- The cross-functional teams work together as a single unit.

- Close communication with the user representative to understand the features.

- Has a definite timeline of maximum one month.

- Instead of doing the entire "thing" at a time, Scrum does a little of everything at a given interval.

- Resources capability and availability are considered before committing anything.

To understand this methodology well, it's important to understand the key terminologies in SCRUM.

Important SCRUM Terminologies

Scrum Team

The scrum team is a team comprising of 7 with + or – two members. These members are a mixture of competencies and comprise of developers, testers, database people, support people etc. along with the product owner and a scrum master.

All these members work together in close collaboration for a recursive and definite interval, to develop and implement the said features. SCRUM team sitting arrangement plays a very important role in their interaction; they never sit in cubicles or cabins, but a huge table.

Sprint

Sprint is a predefined interval or time frame in which the work has to be completed and make it ready for review or ready for production deployment. This time box usually lies between 2 weeks to 1 month.

In our day to day life when we say that we follow 1-month Sprint cycle, it simply means that we work for one month on the tasks and make it ready for review by the end of that month.

Product Owner

The product owner is the key stakeholder or the lead user of the application to be developed. The product owner is the person who represents the customer side. He/she has the final authority and should always be available for the team.

He/she should be reachable when anyone has any doubts that need clarification. It is important for the product owner to understand and not to assign any new requirement in the middle of the sprint or when the sprint has already started.

Scrum Master

Scrum Master is the facilitator of the scrum team. He/she makes sure that the scrum team is productive and progressive. In case of any impediments, scrum master follows up and resolves them for the team. SCRUM Master is the mediator between the PO and the team.

He/she keeps the PO informed about the progress of the Sprint. If there are any roadblocks or concerns for the team, discusses with the PO and gets them resolved. Like the team's Daily Standup, a standup of the SCRUM Master with the PO happens every day.

Business Analyst (BA)

A Business Analyst plays a very important role in SCRUM. This person is responsible for getting the requirement finalized and drafted in the requirement docs (based on which the user stories are created).

If there are any ambiguities in the User Stories / Acceptance criteria, he/she is the one who is approached by the technical (SCRUM) team and he then takes it up to the PO or else if possible resolves on his own. In large scale projects, there may be more than 1 BA but in small-scale projects, the SCRUM Master may be acting as the BA as well.

It is always a good practice to have a BA when the project kick starts.

User Story

User stories are nothing but the requirements or feature which has to be implemented.

In the scrum, we don't have those huge requirements documents, rather the requirements are defined in a single paragraph, typically having the format as:

As a <User / type of user>

You want to <Some achievable goal/target>

To achieve <some result or reason for doing the thing>

For Example: As an Admin you want to have a password lock in case the user enters an incorrect password for 3 consecutive times to restrict unauthorized access.

There are some characteristics of user stories which should be adhered. The user stories should be short, realistic, could be estimated, complete, negotiable and testable. A user story is never altered or changed in the middle of the Sprint.

It is the responsibility of the SCRUM Master and the BA (if applicable) to make sure that the PO has drafted the User Stories correctly with a proper set of the Acceptance Criteria". If any changes which will impact the sprint release are to be made, then such stories are pulled out of the sprint or they are done as per the hours available.

Every user story has an acceptance criterion which should be well defined and understood by the team.

Acceptance criteria details down the user story that provides the supporting documents. It helps to further refine the user story. Anybody from the team can write down the acceptance criteria. Testing team bases their test cases/conditions on these acceptance criteria.

Epics

Epics are equivocal user stories or we can say that these are the user stories which are not defined and are kept for future sprints.

Just try to relate it with life, imagine you are going for a vacation. As you are going next week, you have everything in place like your hotel bookings, sightseeing, travelers check, etc. But what about your vacation plan for next year? You only have a vague idea that you may go to XYZ place, but you have no detailed plan.

An Epic is just like you next year's vacation plan, where you just know that you may want to go, but where, when, with whom, all these details you have no idea at this point of time.

In a similar way, there are features which are required to be implemented in the future whose details are not yet known. Mostly a feature begins with an Epic and then is broken down to stories which could be implemented.

Product Backlog

The product backlog is a kind of bucket or source where all the user stories are kept. This is maintained by the Product Owner. The product backlog can be imagined as a wishlist of the product owner who prioritizes it as per the business needs.

During the planning meeting, one user story is taken from the product backlog, and then the team does the brainstorming, understands it and refines it and collectively decides which user stories to take, with the intervention of the product owner.

Sprint Backlog

Based on the priority, user stories are taken from the Product Backlog as one at a time. The Scrum team brainstorm on it determines the feasibility and decides on the stories to work on a particular sprint. The collective list of all the user stories which the scrum team works on a particular sprint is known as Sprint backlog.

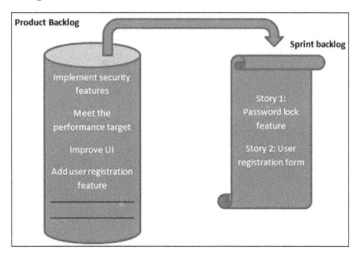

Story Points

Story points are a quantitative indication of the complexity of a user story. Based on the story point, estimation and efforts for a story are determined.

A story point is relative and not absolute. In order to make sure that our estimate and efforts are correct, it's important to check that the user stories are not big. The more precise and smaller is the user story, the more accurate will be the estimation.

Each and every user story is assigned to a story point based on the Fibonacci series (1, 2, 3, 5, 8, 13 & 21). Higher is the number, the complex is the story.

To be precise:

- If you give 1 / 2 / 3 story point it means that the story is small and of low complexity,
- If you give points as 5 / 8, it is a medium complex,
- 13 and 21 are highly complex.

Here complexity consists of both development plus testing effort.

To decide a story point, brainstorming happens within the scrum team and the team collectively decides a story point.

It may happen that the development team gives a story point of 3 to a particular story, because for them it may be 3 lines of code change, but the testing team gives 8 story point because they feel that this code change will affect larger modules so the testing effort would be larger. Whatever story point you are giving, you have to justify it.

So in this situation, brainstorming happens and the team collectively agrees to one story point.

Whenever you are deciding on a story point, keep the below factors in mind:

- The dependency of the story with other application/module.
- The skill-set of the resource.
- The complexity of the story.
- Historical learning.
- Acceptance criteria of the user story.

If you are not aware of a particular story, don't size it.

Whenever a story is = or > 8 points, it is broken down into 2 or more stories.

Burn Down Chart

Burn down chart is a graph which shows the estimated v/s actual effort of the scrum tasks.

It is a tracking mechanism by which for a particular sprint the day to day tasks are tracked to check whether the stories are progressing towards the completion of the committed story points or not.

Example: To understand this, check the figure:

Story	Task	start	Day 1	Day 2	Day 3	Day 4	Day 5	Day 6	Day 7	Day 8	Day 9	Day 10
User story 1	Task 1	8	7	6	5	4	3					
User story 1	Task 2	6	4	4	3	3	22					
User story 1	Task 3	3	3	3	3	2	1					

User story 2	Task 4	7	5	3	2	3	3					
User story 2	Task 5	5	5	4	3	4	4					
User story 2	Task 6	4	4	4	5	3	3					
User story 3	Task 7	9	9	7	8	6	5					
User story 3	Task 8	6	6	6	6	5	4					
User story 4	Task 9	7	5	4	5	3	3					
User story 4	Task 10	8	8	8	7	8	4					
User story 4	Task 11	7	7	7	4	4	4					
Estimated effort		70	63	56	49	42	35	28	21	14	7	0
Actual effort left		70	63	56	51	45	36	0	0	0	0	0

We have assumed:

- 2 weeks Sprint (10 days).

- 2 resources actual working on the sprint.

- "Story": This column shows the user stories taken for the sprint.

- "Task": This column shows the list of the task associated with the user story.

- "Effort": This column shows the effort. Now, this measure is the total effort to complete the task. It does not depict the effort put in by any specific individual.

- "Day 1 – Day 10": This column(s) shows the hours which are left to complete the story. Please see that the hour is NOT the hour which is already done BUT the hours which are still left.

- "Estimated Effort": Is the total of the effort. For the "Start" it is simply the sum of the entire individual task: SUM (C5: C15).

A total number of effort that has to be completed in 1 day is 70 / 10 = 7. So at the end of day 1, the effort should reduce to 70 – 7 = 63. In a similar way, it is calculated for all the days till day 10, when the estimated effort should be 0 (Row 16).

- "Actual Effort Left": As the name suggests, is the effort actually left to complete the story. It may also happen that the actual efforts increases or decreases than the estimated one.

You can use the inbuilt functions and Chart in Excel to create this burndown chart.

Burn Down Chart steps would be:

- Enter all the stories (Column A5 – A15).

- Enter all the Tasks (Column B5 – B15).

- Enter the Days (Day 1 – Day 10).

- Enter the starting efforts (Sum the tasks C5 – C15).

- Apply the formula to calculate the "Estimated Efforts" for each day (Day 1 to Day 10). Enter the formula at D15 (C16-C16/10) and drag it for all the days.

- For each day, enter the actual efforts. Enter the formula at D17 (SUM (D5:D15)) for summing up the actual efforts left, and drag it for all the other days.

- Select it and create the chart as follows:

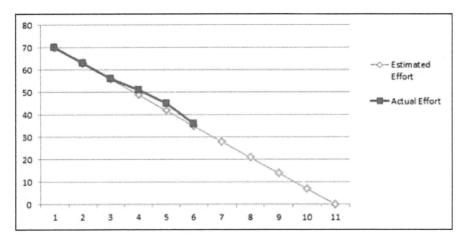

Velocity

The total number of story point which a scrum team archives in a sprint, is called Velocity. The Scrum team is judged or referenced by its velocity. Having said that, it should be kept in mind that the objective here is NOT achieving the maximum story points, but to have a quality deliverable, respecting the scrum team's comfort level.

For Example: For a particular sprint: the total number of user stories are 8 having story points as shown below.

S. No	User Story	Story Points
1	Story 1	3
2	Story 2	5
3	Story 3	2
4	Story 4	3
5	Story 5	8
6	Story 6	5
7	Story 7	1
8	Story 8	3

So here the velocity will be the sum of the story points = 30.

Definition of Done

A Sprint is marked as Done when all the stories are completed, all done, research, QA tasks are marked 'Completed', all bugs are fixed-closed else the ones that can be done later (like not completely related or are less important) are pulled out and added in the backlog, the code review and unit testing is completed, the estimated hours have met the actual hours put up in the tasks and most importantly a successful demo has been given to the PO and the stakeholders.

Activities Done in SCRUM Methodology

Planning Meeting

A planning meeting is the starting point of Sprint. It is the meeting where the entire scrum team gathers, the SCRUM Master selects a user story based on the priority from the product backlog and the team brainstorms on it.

Based on the discussion, the scrum team decides the complexity of the story and sizes it as per the Fibonacci series. The team identifies the tasks along with the efforts (in hours) which would be done to complete the implementation of the user story.

Many a time, the planning meeting is preceded by a "Pre-Planning meeting". It's just like home-work which the scrum team does before they sit for the formal planning meet. The team tries to write down the dependencies or other factors which they would like to discuss in the planning meeting.

Executions of Sprint Tasks

As the name suggests, these are the actual work done by the scrum team to accomplish their task and take the user story into the "Done" state.

Daily Stand-up

During the sprint cycle, every day the scrum team meets for, not more than 15 minutes (could be a stand-up call, recommended to have during the beginning of the day) and state 3 points:

- What did the team member do yesterday?

- What did the team member plan to do today?

- Any impediments (roadblocks)?

It is the Scrum master who facilitates this meeting. In case, any team member is facing any kind of difficulties, the scrum master follows up to get it resolved. In Stand ups, the board is also reviewed and in itself shows the progress of the team.

Review Meeting

At the end of every sprint cycle, the SCRUM team meets again and demonstrates the implemented user stories to the product owner. The product owner may cross verify the stories as per its acceptance criteria. It's again the responsibility of the Scrum master to preside over this meeting.

Also in the SCRUM tool, the Sprint is closed and the tasks are marked done.

Retrospective Meeting

The retrospective meeting happens after the review meeting. The SCRUM team meets, discusses & document the following points:

- What went well during the Sprint (Best practices)?

- What did not go well in the Sprint?

- Lessons learned.

- Action Items.

The Scrum team should continue to follow the best practice, ignore the "not best practices" and implement the lessons learned during the consequent sprints. The retrospective meeting helps to implement the continuous improvement of the SCRUM process.

How the Process is done?

Example:

Step 1: Let's have a SCRUM team of 9 people comprising of 1 product owner, 1 Scrum master, 2 testers, 4 developers and 1 DBA.

Step 2: The Sprint is decided to follow a 4 weeks cycle. So we have 1-month Sprint starting 5th June to 4th of July.

Step 3: The Product Owner has the prioritized list of user stories in the product backlog.

Step 4: The team decides to meet on 4th June for the "Pre Planning" meeting.

- The product owner takes 1 story from the product backlog, describes it and leaves it to the team to brainstorm on it.

- The entire team discusses and communicates directly to the product owner to have clearly understood the user story.

- In a similar way, various other user stories are taken. If possible, the team can go ahead and size the stories as well.

After all the discussion, Individual team members go back to their workstations and,

- Identify their individual tasks for each story.

- Calculate the exact number of hours on which they will be working. Let's check how the member concludes these hours.

  - Total number of working hours = 9

  - Minus 1 hour for a break, minus 1 hour for meetings, minus 1 hour for emails, discussions, troubleshooting etc.

- So the actual working hours = 6.

- A total number of working days during the Sprint = 21 days.

- Total number of hours available = 21*6 = 126.

- The member is on leave for 2 days = 12 hours (This varies for each member, some may take leave and some may not.)

- Number of actual hours = 126 − 12 = 114 hours.

This means that the member will actually be available for 114 hours for this sprint. So he will break down his individual sprint task in such a way that a total of 114 hours is reached.

Step 5: On the 5th of June the entire Scrum team meets for the "Planning Meeting".

- The final verdict of the user story from the product backlog is done and the story is moved to the Sprint Backlog.

- For each story, each team member declares their identified tasks, if required they can have a discussion on those tasks, can size or resize it (remember the Fibonacci series!!).

- The Scrum master or the team enter their individual tasks along with their hours for each story in a tool.

- After all the stories are completed, Scrum master notes the initial Velocity and formally starts the Sprint.

Step 6: Once the Sprint has started, based on the tasks assigned, each team member starts working on those tasks.

Step 7: The team meets daily for 15 minutes and discusses 3 things:

- What did they do yesterday?

- What they plan to do today?

- Any impediments (roadblocks)?

Step 8: The scrum master tracks the progress on a daily basis with the help of "Burn down chart".

Step 9: In case of any impediments, the Scrum master follows up to resolve those.

Step 10: On 4th July, the team meets again for the review meeting. A member demonstrates the implemented user story to the product owner.

Step 11: On 5th July, the Team meets again for the Retrospective, where they discuss:

- What went well?

- What did not go well?

- Action Items.

Step 12: On 6th July, the Team again meets for pre-planning meeting for the next sprint and the cycle continues.

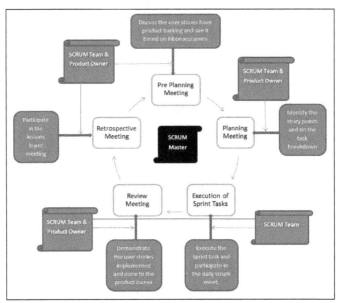

SCRUM Process

SCRUM Activity Tools

There are several tools that can be used extensively for tracking scrum activities.

Some of them include:

- Jira
- XPlanner
- VersionOne
- Sprintometer
- ScrumNinja

References

- Introduction-software-development-methodologies: alliancesoftware.com.au, Retrieved 2 February, 2019
- What-is-sdlc-waterfall-model: softwaretestinghelp.com, Retrieved 11 April, 2019
- Agile: agilealliance.org, Retrieved 14 July, 2019
- Agile-methodology: stackify.com, Retrieved 5 May, 2019
- Agile-scrum-extreme-testing: guru99.com, Retrieved 15 February, 2019
- Software-engineering-spiral-model: geeksforgeeks.org, Retrieved 20 March, 2019
- Sdlc_iterative_model: tutorialspoint.com, Retrieved 2 August, 2019
- Agile-scrum-methodology-for-development-and-testing: softwaretestinghelp.com, Retrieved 22 June, 2019

3

Feasibility Study

The study which evaluates the practicality and viability of the software solution that is being considered to fulfill the requirements is known as a feasibility study. The topics elaborated in this chapter will help in gaining a better perspective about different facets which are examined in feasibility studies such as economic and technical feasibility.

Feasibility is defined as the practical extent to which a project can be performed successfully. To evaluate feasibility, a feasibility study is performed, which determines whether the solution considered to accomplish the requirements is practical and workable in the software. Information such as resource availability, cost estimation for software development, benefits of the software to the organization after it is developed and cost to be incurred on its maintenance are considered during the feasibility study. The objective of the feasibility study is to establish the reasons for developing the software that is acceptable to users, adaptable to change and conformable to established standards. Various other objectives of feasibility study are listed below.

- To analyze whether the software will meet organizational requirements.

- To determine whether the software can be implemented using the current technology and within the specified budget and schedule.

- To determine whether the software can be integrated with other existing software.

Types of Feasibility

Various types of feasibility that are commonly considered include technical feasibility, operational feasibility, and economic feasibility.

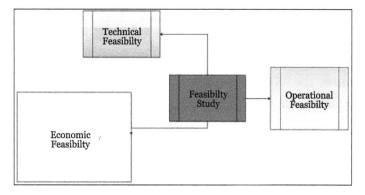

Technical feasibility assesses the current resources (such as hardware and software) and technology, which are required to accomplish user requirements in the software within the allocated time and budget. For this, the software development team ascertains whether the current resources and technology can be upgraded or added in the software to accomplish specified user requirements. Technical feasibility also performs the following tasks.

- Analyzes the technical skills and capabilities of the software development team members.

- Determines whether the relevant technology is stable and established.

- Ascertains that the technology chosen for software development has a large number of users so that they can be consulted when problems arise or improvements are required.

Operational feasibility assesses the extent to which the required software performs a series of steps to solve business problems and user requirements. This feasibility is dependent on human resources (software development team) and involves visualizing whether the software will operate after it is developed and be operative once it is installed. Operational feasibility also performs the following tasks.

- Determines whether the problems anticipated in user requirements are of high priority.

- Determines whether the solution suggested by the software development team is acceptable.

- Analyzes whether users will adapt to a new software.

- Determines whether the organization is satisfied by the alternative solutions proposed by the software development team.

Economic feasibility determines whether the required software is capable of generating financial gains for an organization. It involves the cost incurred on the software development team, estimated cost of hardware and software, cost of performing feasibility study, and so on. For this, it is essential to consider expenses made on purchases (such as hardware purchase) and activities required to carry out software development. In addition, it is necessary to consider the benefits that can be achieved by developing the software. Software is said to be economically feasible if it focuses on the issues listed below.

- Cost incurred on software development to produce long-term gains for an organization.

- Cost required conducting full software investigation (such as requirements elicitation and requirements analysis).

- Cost of hardware, software, development team, and training.

Feasibility Study Process

Feasibility study comprises the following steps:

- Information assessment: Identifies information about whether the system helps in achieving the objectives of the organization. It also verifies that the system can be implemented using new technology and within the budget and whether the system can be integrated with the existing system.

- Information collection: Specifies the sources from where information about software can be obtained. Generally, these sources include users (who will operate the software), organization (where the software will be used), and the software development team (which understands user requirements and knows how to fulfill them in software).

- Report writing: Uses a feasibility report, which is the conclusion of the feasibility study by the software development team. It includes the recommendations whether the software development should continue. This report may also include information about changes in the software scope, budget, and schedule and suggestions of any requirements in the system.

- General information: Describes the purpose and scope of feasibility study. It also describes system overview, project references, acronyms and abbreviations, and points of contact to be used. System overview provides description about the name of the organization responsible for the software development, system name or title, system category, operational status, and so on. Project references provide a list of the references used to prepare this document such as documents relating to the project or previously developed documents that are related to the project. Acronyms and abbreviations provide a list of the terms that are used in this document along with their meanings. Points of contact provide a list of points of organizational contact with users for information and coordination. For example, users require assistance to solve problems (such as troubleshooting) and collect information such as contact number, e-mail address, and so on.

Management summary provides the following information:

- Environment: Identifies the individuals responsible for software development. It provides information about input and output requirements, processing requirements of the software and the interaction of the software with other software. It also identifies system security requirements and the system's processing requirements.

- Current functional procedures: Describes the current functional procedures of the existing system, whether automated or manual. It also includes the data-flow of the current system and the number of team members required to operate and maintain the software.

- Functional objective: Provides information about functions of the system such as new services, increased capacity, and so on.

- Performance objective: Provides information about performance objectives such as reduced staff and equipment costs, increased processing speeds of software, and improved controls.

- Assumptions and constraints: Provides information about assumptions and constraints such as operational life of the proposed software, financial constraints, changing hardware, software and operating environment, and availability of information and sources.

- Methodology: Describes the methods that are applied to evaluate the proposed software in order to reach a feasible alternative. These methods include survey, modeling, benchmarking, etc.

- Evaluation criteria: Identifies criteria such as cost, priority, development time, and ease of system use, which are applicable for the development process to determine the most suitable system option.

- Recommendation: Describes a recommendation for the proposed system. This includes the delays and acceptable risks.

- Proposed software: Describes the overall concept of the system as well as the procedure to be used to meet user requirements. In addition, it provides information about improvements, time and resource costs, and impacts. Improvements are performed to enhance the functionality and performance of the existing software. Time and resource costs include the costs associated with software development from its requirements to its maintenance and staff training. Impacts describe the possibility of future happenings and include various types of impacts as listed below.

  ○ Equipment impacts: Determine new equipment requirements and changes to be made in the currently available equipment requirements.

  ○ Software impacts: Specify any additions or modifications required in the existing software and supporting software to adapt to the proposed software.

  ○ Organizational impacts: Describe any changes in organization, staff and skills requirement.

  ○ Operational impacts: Describe effects on operations such as user-operating procedures, data processing, data entry procedures, and so on.

  ○ Developmental impacts: Specify developmental impacts such as resources required to develop databases, resources required to develop and test the software, and specific activities to be performed by users during software development.

  ○ Security impacts: Describe security factors that may influence the development, design, and continued operation of the proposed software.

  ○ Alternative systems: Provide description of alternative systems, which are considered in a feasibility study. This also describes the reasons for choosing a particular alternative system to develop the proposed software and the reason for rejecting alternative systems.

Economic and Technical Feasibility

Economic Feasibility

Economic evaluation is a vital part of investment appraisal, dealing with factors that can be quantified, measured, and compared in monetary terms the results of an economic evaluation are considered with other aspects to make the project investment decision as the proper investment appraisal helps to ensure that the right project is undertaken in a manner that gives it the best chances of success.

Project investments involve the expenditure of capital funds and other resources to generate future benefits, whether in the form of profits, cost savings, or social benefits. For an investment to be worthwhile, the future benefit should compare favourably with the prior expenditure of resources need to achieve them.

Cost/Benefit Analysis

To assess economic feasibility, management has to analyze costs and benefits associated with the proposed project. The capital cost of a project affects the economic evaluation. Cost estimating is essentially an intuitive process that attempts to predict the final outcome of a future capital expenditure. Even though it seem impossible to come up with the exact number of costs and benefits for a particular project during this initial phase of the development process, one should spend the adequate of time in estimating the costs and benefits of the project for comparison with other alternatives.

When talking about the cost of IT/IS project, one would first think of the tangible costs that are easily to determine and estimate, such as hardware and software cost, or labor cost. However, in addition to these tangible costs, there are also some intangible costs, such as loss of goodwill, or operational inefficiency.

One methodology for determining the costs of implementing and maintaining information technology is Total Cost of Ownership (TCO). It is a financial estimate designed to help consumers and enterprise managers assess direct and indirect costs. Bill Kirwin, VP and Research director of Gartner stated that "TCO is a holistic assessment of IT costs over time. The term holistic assessment implies an all-encompassing collection of the costs associated with IT investments, including capital investment, license fees, leasing costs, and service fees, as well as direct (budgeted) and indirect(unbudgeted) labor expenses". An advisory firm Garter, Inc. has identified and offered statement on the financial impact of deploying information technology during its whole life-cycle as following:

- End-user computer Hardware purchase costs,
- Software license purchase costs,
- Hardware & Software deployment costs,
- Hardware warranties and maintenance costs,
- Software license tracking costs,
- Operations Infrastructure Costs,
- Cost of Security Breaches (in loss of reputation and recovery cost),
- Cost for electricity and cooling,
- Network hardware and software costs,
- Server hardware and software costs,
- Insurance costs,
- Testing costs,
- Cost to upgrade or scalability,
- IT Personnel costs,
- "C" Level Management Time costs,

- Backup and Recovery Process costs,
- Costs associated with failure or outage,
- Diminished performance incidents (i.e. users having to wait),
- Technology training costs of users and IT staff,
- Infrastructure (floor space) costs,
- Audit costs,
- Migration costs.

On the other hand, IT/IS projects can provide many benefits, both tangible and intangible, to an organization. The tangible benefit, such as cost saving or increasing in revenue, would be easier to estimate while intangible benefits are harder to quantify.

Time Value of Money

There are several economic evaluation methods available to assess an investment. The most widely used methods are Net Present Value (NPV) and Discounted Cash Flow Rate of Return, or Internal Rate of Return (IRR). Even though, NPV approach and IRR approach will normally provide the same decision result, polls of industry indicate that the IRR is the number one economic evaluation decision method use by about two-thirds of industrial companies. This is due to the fact that some managers prefer a percentage rate of return more than the dollar amount from NPV.

Before calculating NPV and IRR, one should have an understanding of basic finance concept called "Time value of money". The concept of Time value of money is that a dollar today is worth more than a dollar available at a future date because a dollar today can be invested and earn a return. Someone investing a sum of money today at a given interest rate for a given period of time would expect to have larger sum of money at the future date. As different projects may provide benefits at the different time in the future, all costs and benefits of the projects should be viewed in relation to their present value.

Present value is the value of a future cash stream discounted at the appropriate market interest rate, called discount rate. The present value of the future cash flow can be calculated using the following equation:

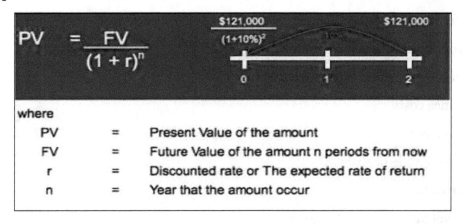

$$PV = \frac{FV}{(1 + r)^n}$$

where

PV	=	Present Value of the amount
FV	=	Future Value of the amount n periods from now
r	=	Discounted rate or The expected rate of return
n	=	Year that the amount occur

Net Present Value (NPV) and Internal Rate of Return (IRR)

	Net Present Value (NPV)	Internal Rate of Return (IRR)
Concept	Adding the present values of each individual positive or negative cash flow based on the opportunity cost of capital. In this case the present is taken as the time at which evaluation is carried out.	The discount rate at which the net present value of an investment is zero.
Decision Rule	For independent projects, • Accept if NPV is greater than zero. • Reject if NPV is less than zero. • For mutually exclusive projects (choose one project over others), accept the project with the highest positive NPV.	For independent projects, • Accept if IRR is equal or greater than required rate of return. • Reject if IRR is less than required rate of return. • For mutually exclusive projects, accept the project with the highest IRR that is greater than required rate of return.
Strengths	• NPV is a direct measure of a project's dollar benefit. • NPV approach fully accounts for time value of money and considers all cash flow over the life of the project. • NPV assumes that firms can reinvest all of the cash inflow at the project's required rate of return throughout the life of the project. This rate is more realistic than the IRR rate. • NPV approach provides the accept-reject decision for both independent and mutually exclusive project.	• IRR measures profitability as a percentage showing the return on each dollar invested. • IRR approach fully accounts for time value of money and considers all cash flow over the life of the project. • IRR provides the safety margin information to management. Thus, the higher IRR is the safety margin. • Some managers prefer the IRR because they like dealing with the percentage rates of return more than with the dollar value in NPV.
Weaknesses	• NPV does not provide a gauge for relative profitability. For example, NPV $1,000 is highly desirable for a project costing $2,000 but not for a project coating $1 million. NPV only provide the total profits gained, but not the percentage gained. • Some people have difficulty understanding the meaning of NPV measure. Therefore, in practice, managers often prefer a percentage return to a PV of dollar return.	• IRR method can provide no IRR or multiple IRRs if a project has a non-conventional cash flow pattern, such as, cash flow pattern has more than one sign change (-/+/-). • IRR assumes that firms can reinvest all of the cash inflow at the IRR rate throughout the life of the project. This rate may be unrealistic. • IRR may lead to inconsistence of ranking for mutually exclusive projects as it does not provide the magnitude or duration of its cash flow.

Break-Even Analysis

Break-even analysis is a type of cost benefit analysis to identify at what point (if ever) benefits equal costs.

$$\text{Break-Even Ratio} \quad = \quad \frac{\text{Yearly NPV Cash Flow} \;-\; \text{Overall NPV Cash Flow}}{\text{Yearly NPV Cash Flow}}$$

The break-even point is usually expressed as the amount of revenue that must be realized for the firm to have neither profit nor loss. It expresses a minimum revenue target. (Marshall, McManus, and Viele) It can be expressed in numbers or by the use of graphs.

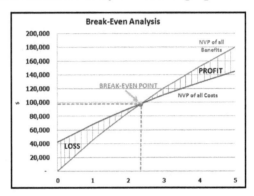

An Example of Economic Valuation Method

A system analysts estimate the cost for the new system as $42,500 onetime investment for developing, updating hardware, and user training. Also, firm needs to pay $28,500 each year for software maintenance, incremental communication cost, and supplies. On the other hand, the system will provide approximately $50,000 per year. Assume the expected rate of return (discount rate) is 12%.

Net economic benefits		50,000	50,000	50,000	50,000	50,000
Net cost	(42,500)	(28,500)	(28,500)	(28,500)	(28,500)	(28,500)
Net cash flow each year	(42,500)	21,500	21,500	21,500	21,500	21,500
Year	0	1	2	3	4	5

After determining costs and benefits of a new system, the system analysts evaluate the project using NPV, IRR, Break-even analysis, or other methods. Also, using a time diagram is helpful to illustrate the timing of cash flows, especially for situations involving cash flows at the different points in time that are not equal.

NPV = PV of total benefits − PV of total costs

$$= -42500 + \frac{21,500}{1.12} + \frac{21,500}{1.12^2} + \frac{21,500}{1.12^3} + \frac{21,500}{1.12^4} + \frac{21,500}{1.12^5}$$

$$= 35,003 \quad \text{(Accept this project as NPV > 0)}$$

IRR = Discount rate that NPV = 0

$$= -42500 + \frac{21,500}{(1+r)} + \frac{21,500}{(1+r)^2} + \frac{21,500}{(1+r)^3} + \frac{21,500}{(1+r)^4} + \frac{21,500}{(1+r)^5}$$

$$= 41.75\% \quad \text{(Accept this project as IRR > 12%)}$$

Break-Even analysis						
Year	0	1	2	3	4	5
Yearly NPV	(42,500)	19,196	17,140	15,303	13,664	12,200
Overall NPV	(42,500)	(23,304)	(6,164)	9,139	22,803	35,003

Thus, the project breakeven occurs around year 3.

Break-Even Ratio at year 3 = (15,303 - 9,139) / 15,303 = 0.403

Other Economic Feasibility Methods

Also, there are other financial methods that are used to evaluate the project investment:

- Return on investment (ROI) equals to net cash receipts of the project divided by the cash outlays of the project. Firms choose the project that provides the highest ROI.

- Payback period (PP) is amount of time required for an investment to generate sufficient cash flows to recover its initial cost. Payback period is similar to the break-even analysis, except the fact that payback period ignores the concept of time value of money.

- Profitability index (PI) shows the relative profitability of any investment. It equal to the present value of cash inflow divided by present value of cash outflow.

Technical Feasibility

Assessing technical feasibility is to evaluate whether the new system will perform adequately and whether an organization has ability to construct a proposed system or not. The technical assessment help answer the question such as whether the technology needed for the system exists, how difficult it will be to build, and whether the firm has enough experience using that technology. One examples of the technical feasibility is shown in the credit union management.

- "It worked great and clients were happy with it and felt that it met their needs, but obviously that platform needed to be upgraded to meet the current technology direction for the industry. It was no longer going to be supportable long-term" said Sara L. Brooks, chief strategy officer for Fiserv's credit union division.

- Even though a particular operating system may run on different computer architectures, the software written for that operating system may not automatically work on all architectures that the operating system supports. For example, in 2006, OpenOffice.org did not natively run on the processors implementing the 64-bits standards for computers. Therefore, implementing the Open Office at that time would not be feasible in technical term if the company have 64-bits computer architectures.

In developing the new system, one has to investigate and compare technology providers, determine reliability and competitiveness of that system, and identify limitations or constraints of technology, as well as the risk of the proposed system that is depend on the size of the system, complexity, and group's experience with the similar systems.

- Project Size: Project size can be determined by the number of members on the project team, project duration time, number of department involved, or the effort put in programming. (Hoffer, George, and Valacich) The larger the size of the projects, the riskier the project is. The CHAOS Report confirms that small projects are more likely to succeed than large projects. "The smaller the team and the shorter the duration of the project, the greater the *likelihood of success."*

Project Size	People	Time	Success Rate
Less than $ 750k	6	6	55%
$750k to $ 1.5M	12	9	33%
$ 1.5M to $3m	25	12	25%
$ 3M to $ 6m	40	18	15%
$ 6M to $ 10m	250	24	8%
Over $10m	500	36	0%

- Project Structure: The project that its requirements are highly structured and well define will have lower risk than the one that the requirements are subject to the judgment of an individual.

- Familiarity with Technology or Application area: The project will be less risky if the development and the user group is familiar with the technology and the systems. Therefore, it would be less risky if the development team uses the standard development tool and hardware environments. Also, on the users' side, the more users familiar with the systems development process, the more likely they understand the need for their involvement; this involvement can lead to the success of the project.

However, one thing to keep in mind is that a project with the highly risk may still be conducted. Most company would have the reasonable combination among high-, medium-, and low-risk projects. Without the high-risk project, the organization couldn't make the major breakthroughs in innovative uses of systems.

Prototyping

Prototyping is defined as the process of developing a working replication of a product or system that has to be engineered. It offers a small scale facsimile of the end product and is used for obtaining customer feedback as described below.

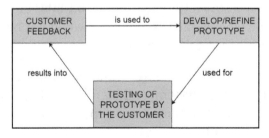

The Prototyping Model is one of the most popularly used Software Development Life Cycle Models

(SDLC models).This model is used when the customers do not know the exact project requirements beforehand. In this model, a prototype of the end product is first developed, tested and refined as per customer feedback repeatedly till a final acceptable prototype is achieved which forms the basis for developing the final product.

In this process model, the system is partially implemented before or during the analysis phase thereby giving the customers an opportunity to see the product early in the life cycle. The process starts by interviewing the customers and developing the incomplete high-level paper model. This document is used to build the initial prototype supporting only the basic functionality as desired by the customer. Once the customer figures out the problems, the prototype is further refined to eliminate them. The process continues till the user approves the prototype and finds the working model to be satisfactory.

There are 2 approaches for this model:

- Rapid Throwaway Prototyping: This technique offers a useful method of exploring ideas and getting customer feedback for each of them. In this method, a developed prototype need not necessarily be a part of the ultimately accepted prototype. Customer feedback helps in preventing unnecessary design faults and hence, the final prototype developed is of a better quality.

- Evolutionary Prototyping: In this method, the prototype developed initially is incrementally refined on the basis of customer feedback till it finally gets accepted. In comparison to Rapid Throwaway Prototyping, it offers a better approach which saves time as well as effort. This is because developing a prototype from scratch for every iteration of the process can sometimes be very frustrating for the developers.

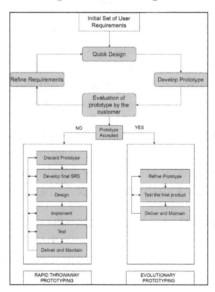

Necessity of the Prototyping Model

- It is advantageous to develop the Graphical User Interface (GUI) part of software using the Prototyping Model. Through prototype, the user can experiment with a working user interface and they can suggest any change if needed.

- The prototyping model is especially useful when the exact technical solutions are unclear to the development team. A prototype can help them to critically examine the technical issues associated with the product development. The lack of familiarity with a required development technology is a technical risk. This can be resolved by developing a prototype to understand the issues and accommodate the changes in the next iteration.

Phases of Prototyping Model

The Prototyping Model of software development is graphically shown in the figure below. The software is developed through two major activities – one is prototype construction and another is iterative waterfall based software development.

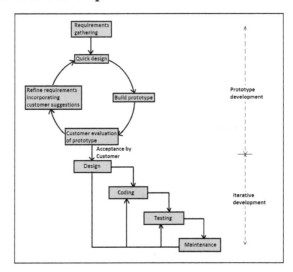

- Prototype Development: Prototype development starts with an initial requirements gathering phase. A quick design is carried out and a prototype is built. The developed prototype is submitted to the customer for evaluation. Based on the customer feedback, the requirements are refined and the prototype is suitably modified. This cycle of obtaining customer feedback and modifying the prototype continues till the customer approves the prototype.

- Iterative Development: Once the customer approves the prototype, the actual software is developed using the iterative waterfall approach. In spite of the availability of a working prototype, the SRS document is usually needed to be developed since the SRS Document is invaluable for carrying out tractability analysis, verification and test case design during later phases.

The code for the prototype is usually thrown away. However, the experience gathered from developing the prototype helps a great deal in developing the actual software. By constructing the prototype and submitting it for user evaluation, many customer requirements get properly defined and technical issues get resolved by experimenting with the prototype. This minimises later change requests from the customer and the associated redesign costs.

Advantages

- The customers get to see the partial product early in the life cycle. This ensures a greater level of customer satisfaction and comfort.

- New requirements can be easily accommodated as there is scope for refinement.

- Missing functionalities can be easily figured out.

- Errors can be detected much earlier thereby saving a lot of effort and cost, besides enhancing the quality of the software.

- The developed prototype can be reused by the developer for more complicated projects in the future.

- Flexibility in design.

Disadvantages

- Costly w.r.t time as well as money.

- There may be too much variation in requirements each time the prototype is evaluated by the customer.

- Poor Documentation due to continuously changing customer requirements.

- It is very difficult for the developers to accommodate all the changes demanded by the customer.

- There is uncertainty in determining the number of iterations that would be required before the prototype is finally accepted by the customer.

- After seeing an early prototype, the customers sometimes demand the actual product to be delivered soon.

- Developers in a hurry to build prototypes may end up with sub-optimal solutions.

- The customer might lose interest in the product if he/she is not satisfied with the initial prototype.

Use

The Prototyping Model should be used when the requirements of the product are not clearly understood or are unstable. It can also be used if requirements are changing quickly. This model can be successfully used for developing user interfaces, high technology software-intensive systems, and systems with complex algorithms and interfaces. It is also a very good choice to demonstrate the technical feasibility of the product.

Pilot Project Testing

Pilot Testing is defined as a type of Software Testing that verifies a component of the system or the entire system under a real-time operating condition. It verifies the major functionality of the system before going into production. This testing is done exactly between the UAT and Production.

In Pilot testing, a selected group of end users try the system under test and provide the feedback before the full deployment of the system. In other words, it means to conduct a dress rehearsal for the usability test that follows.

Pilot Testing helps in early detection of bugs in the System. It is concerned with installing a system on a customer site (or a user simulated environment) for testing against continuous and regular use. The most common method of testing is to continuously test the system to find out its weak areas. These weaknesses are then sent back to the development team as bug reports, and these bugs are fixed in the next build of the system.

During this process sometimes acceptance testing is also included as part of Compatibility Testing. This occurs when a system is being developed to replace an old one.

In Software Engineering, Pilot Testing will answer the question like, whether the product or service has a potential market.

Need for Pilot Testing

The most important objective of Pilot Testing is to debug the software and procedure that will be used for the test.

It will help to check if a product is ready for full-scale implementation:

- It will help to make a better decision on allotment of time and resources.

- It will give an opportunity to gauge a target population's reaction to the program.

- It will help to measure the success of a program.

- It will give the team a chance to uncover and practice the activities they will be using during the usability test.

Steps to do Pilot Testing

The level of Pilot testing depends on the size and scope of a migration project. The actual Pilot testing is done in a dedicated area or lab where users run numerous procedures, transactions, and reports as they simulate the software's functionality.

Pilot testing can be conducted depending on the context of the project:

- For a general business enterprise, a pilot test can be conducted with a group of users on a set of servers in a datacenter.

- For a web development enterprise, a pilot test can be conducted by hosting site files on staging servers or folders live on the internet.

- For commercial software vendors, a pilot test can be conducted with a special group of early adopters.

Pilot testing involves following Test Plan:

- Step 1: Create a Pilot Plan.

- Step 2: Prepare for the Pilot test.
- Step 3: Deploy and test the Pilot test.
- Step 4: Evaluate the Pilot test.
- Step 5: Prepare for production deployment.

Before conducting a Pilot Testing following things need to be considered:

- Provide adequate training to participants.
- A rollout plan for deploying the servers and preparing systems for the pilot.
- Documentation of the installation process.
- Testing scripts for each software application. It consists of checklists of functions to be executed.
- Provide constant feedback to the design and testing teams from users by using emails or websites.
- Set the evaluation criteria for the pilot, like information about the number of users who were dissatisfied, the number of support calls and requests, etc.
- Engage a working group of community partners or stakeholders who have invested in a project and will meet regularly to discuss the progress.
- Developed an evaluation plan and evaluation instruments/tools to capture the necessary information about knowledge, changes in attitudes and behavior of the pilot group.

During the Pilot test, the team gathers and evaluate test data. Based on these data, the team will choose one of the strategies.

- Stagger Forward- Deploy a new release candidate to the pilot group,
- Roll back- Execute the rollback plan to restore the pilot group to its previous configuration state,
- Suspend- Suspend pilot testing,
- Patch and Continue- Deploy patches to fix the existing solution,
- Deploy- Proceed to a deployment of the solution.

Good Practice for Pilot Testing

- Schedule the pilot test two days before the usability test.
- Do not initiate pilot test until all users, customers and project team agree on the criteria for a successful result.
- Ask users to mark any issues on their copies of materials, describe their concerns, and offer suggestions (if they have any) for improvement.
- Inform to users the purpose, length, and progress of the pilot.

References

- Feasibilitystudy: ecomputernotes.com, Retrieved 2 January, 2019

- Katimuneetorn_Feasibility_Study: umsl.edu, Retrieved 22 May, 2019

- Software-engineering-prototyping-model: geeksforgeeks.org, Retrieved 14 August, 2019

- Software-engineering-phases-prototyping-model-set: geeksforgeeks.org, Retrieved 11 March, 2019

- Software-engineering-prototyping-model: geeksforgeeks.org, Retrieved 20 June, 2019

- Pilot-testing: guru99.com, Retrieved 25 April, 2019

Software Requirement Specifications

The document which details what the software will do and how is it expected to perform is known as software requirements specification. Some of the types of software requirements are functional and non-functional requirements. The chapter closely examines these key types of software requirements to provide an extensive understanding of the subject.

Once a system has been deployed, new requirements inevitably emerge. It is difficult for the users to anticipate the effect of these new requirements (if a new system is developed for these requirements) on the organization. Thus, to understand and control changes to system requirements, requirements management is performed.

Requirements management can be defined as a process of eliciting, documenting, organizing, and controlling changes to the requirements. Generally, the process of requirements management begins as soon as the requirements document is available, but 'planning' for managing the changing requirements should start during the requirements elicitation process.

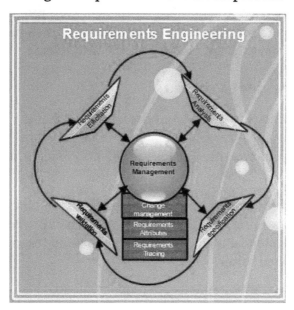

The essential activities performed in requirements management are listed below:

1. Recognizing the need for change in the requirements.

2. Establishing a relationship amongst stakeholders and involving them in the requirements engineering process.

3. Identifying and tracking requirements attributes.

Requirements management enables the development team to identify, control, and track requirements and changes that occur as the software development process progresses. Other advantages associated with the requirements management are listed below;

1. Better control of complex projects: This provides the development team with a clear understanding of what, when, and why the software is to be delivered. The resources are allocated according to user-driven priorities and relative implementation effort.

2. Improved software quality: This ensures that the software performs according to the requirements to enhance software quality. This can be achieved when the developers and testers have a precise understanding of what to develop and test.

3. Reduced project costs and delays: This minimizes errors early in the development cycle as it is expensive to 'fix' errors at the later stages of the development cycle. As a result, the project costs also reduce.

4. Improved team communication: This facilitates early involvement of users to ensure that their needs are achieved.

5. Easing compliance with standards and regulations: This ensures that standards involved with software compliance and process improvement have a thorough understanding of requirements management. For example, CMM addresses requirements management as one of the first steps to improve software quality.

6. All the user requirements are specified in the software requirements specification. The project manager as part of requirements management tracks the requirements for the current project and those which are planned for the next release.

Requirements Management Process

Requirements management starts with planning, which establishes the level of requirements management needed. After planning, each requirement is assigned a unique 'identifier' so that it can be crosschecked by other requirements. Once requirements are identified, requirements tracing is performed.

Requirements tracing is a medium to trace requirements from the start of development process till the software is delivered to the user. The objective of requirements tracing is to ensure that all the requirements are well understood and included in test plans and test cases. Various advantages of requirements tracing are listed below:

1. It verifies whether user requirements are implemented and adequately tested.

2. It enables user understanding of impact of changing requirements.

Trace ability techniques facilitate the impact of analysis on changes of the project, which is under development. Traceability information is stored in a traceability matrix, which relates requirements to stakeholders or design module. The traceability matrix refers to a table that correlates high-level requirements with the detailed requirements of the product. Mainly, five types of traceability tables are maintained. These are listed in table.

In a traceability matrix, each requirement is entered in a row and column of the matrix. The dependencies between different requirements are represented in the cell at a row and column intersection. 'U' in the row and column intersection indicates the dependencies of the requirements in the row on the column and 'R' in the row and column intersection indicates the existence of some other weaker relationship between the requirements.

Table: Types of traceability tables.

Traceability Table	Description
Features traceability	Indicates how requirements relate to important features specified by the user.
Source traceability	Identifies the source of each requirement by linking the requirements to the stakeholders who proposed them. When a change is proposed, information from this table can be used to find and consult the stakeholders.
Requirements traceability	Indicates how dependent requirements in the SRS are related to one another. Information from this table can be used to evaluate the number of requirements that will be affected due to the proposed change(s).
Design traceability	Links the requirements to the design modules where these requirements are implemented. Information from this table can be used to evaluate the impact of proposed requirements changes on the software design and implementation.
Interface traceability	Indicates how requirements are related to internal interface and external interface of a system.

Traceability Matrix

Req. ID	1.1	1.2	1.3	2.1	2.2	2.3	3.1	3.2
1.1		U	R					
1.2			U			R		U
1.3	R			R				
2.1			R		U			U
2.2								U
2.3		R		U				
3.1								R
3.2							R	

Note that a traceability matrix is useful when less number of requirements is to be managed. However, traceability matrices are expensive to maintain when a large system with large requirements is to be developed. This is because large requirements are not easy to manage. Due to this, the traceability information of large system is stored in the 'requirements database' where each requirement is explicitly linked to related requirements. This helps to assess how a change in one requirement affects the different aspects of the system to be developed.

Requirements Change Management

Requirements change management is used when there is a request or proposal for a change in the requirements. The advantage of this process is that the changes to the proposals are managed consistently and in a controlled manner. Note that many activities of requirements management are similar to software configuration management activities.

An efficient requirements change management process undergoes a number of stages for changes to the requirements. These stages are listed below:

1. Problem analysis and change specification: The entire process begins with identification of problems to the requirements. The problem or proposal is analyzed to verify whether

the change is valid. The outcome of the analysis is provided to the 'change requester' and a more specific requirements change proposal is then made.

2. Change analysis and costing: The effect of a change requested on the requirement is assessed according to traceability information. The cost for this can be estimated on the basis of modification made to the design and implementation. After the analysis is over, a decision is made whether changes are to be made.

3. Change implementation: Finally, the changes are made to the requirements document, system design and implementation. The requirements document is organized in such a manner so that changes to it can be made without extensive rewriting. Minimizing the external references and making document sections modular achieves changeability in the document. By doing this, individual sections can be changed and replaced without affecting other parts of the document.

Types of Software Requirements

Requirements help to understand the behavior of a system, which is described by various tasks of the system. For example, some of the tasks of a system are to provide a response to input values, determine the state of data objects, and so on. Note that requirements are considered prior to the development of the software. The requirements, which are commonly considered, are classified into three categories, namely, functional requirements, non-functional requirements, and domain requirements.

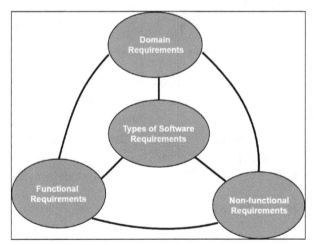

Functional requirement is defined as 'a function that a system or component must be able to perform.' These requirements describe the interaction of software with its environment and specify the inputs, outputs, external interfaces, and the functions that should be included in the software. Also, the services provided byfunctional requirements specify the procedure by which the software should reactto particular inputs or behave in particular situations.

To understand functional requirements properly, let us consider the following example of an online banking system.

1. The user of the bank should be able to search the desired services from the available ones.

2. There should be appropriate documents' for users to read. This implies that when a user wants to open an account in the bank, the forms must be available so that the user can open an account.

3. After registration, the user should be provided with a unique acknowledgement number so that he can later be given an account number.

Functional requirements describe the specific services provided by the online banking system. These requirements indicate user requirements and specify that functional requirements may be described at different levels of detail in an online banking system. With the help of these functional requirements, users can easily view, search and download registration forms and other information about the bank. On the other hand, if requirements are not stated properly, they are misinterpreted by software engineers and user requirements are not met.

The functional requirements should be complete and consistent. Completeness implies that all the user requirements are defined. Consistency implies that all requirements are specified clearly without any contradictory definition. Generally, it is observed that completeness and consistency cannot be achieved in large software or in a complex system due to the problems that arise while defining the functional requirements of these systems. The different needs of stakeholders also prevent the achievement of completeness and consistency. Due to these reasons, requirements may not be obvious when they are, 'first specified and may further lead to inconsistencies in the requirements specification.

The non-functional requirements (also known as quality requirements) are related to system attributes such as reliability and response time. Non-functional requirements arise due to user requirements, budget constraints, organizational policies, and so on. These requirements are not related directly to any particular function provided by the system.

Non-functional requirements should be accomplished in software to make it perform efficiently. For example, if an aeroplane is unable to fulfill reliability requirements, it is not approved for safe operation. Similarly, if a real time control system is ineffective in accomplishing non-functional requirements, the control functions cannot operate correctly.

The description of different types of non-functional requirements is listed below:

1. Product requirements: These requirements specify how software product performs. Product requirements comprise the following.

2. Efficiency requirements: Describe the extent to which the software makes optimal use of resources, the speed with which the system executes, and the memory it consumes for its operation. For example, the system should be able to operate at least three times faster than the existing system.

3. Reliability requirements: Describe the acceptable failure rate of the software. For example, the software should be able to operate even if a hazard occurs.

4. Portability requirements: Describe the ease with which the software can be transferred from one platform to another. For example, it should be easy to port the software to a different operating system without the need to redesign the entire software.

5. Usability requirements: Describe the ease with which users are able to operate the software. For example, the software should be able to provide access to functionality with fewer keystrokes and mouse clicks.

6. Organizational requirements: These requirements are derived from the policies and procedures of an organization. Organizational requirements comprise the following.

7. Delivery requirements: Specify when the software and its documentation are to be delivered to the user.

8. Implementation requirements: Describe requirements such as programming language and design method.

9. Standards requirements: Describe the process standards to be used during software development. For example, the software should be developed using standards specified by the ISO and IEEE standards.

10. External requirements: These requirements include all the requirements that affect the software or its development process externally. External requirements comprise the following.

11. Interoperability requirements: Define the way in which different computer based systems will interact with each other in one or more organizations.

12. Ethical requirements: Specify the rules and regulations of the software so that they are acceptable to users.

13. Legislative requirements: Ensure that the software operates within the legal jurisdiction. For example, pirated software should not be sold.

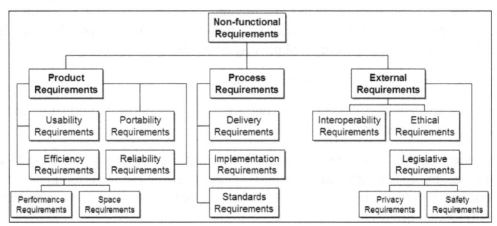

Non-functional requirements are difficult to verify. Hence, it is essential to write non-functional requirements quantitatively, so that they can be tested. For this, non-functional requirements metrics are used. These metrics are listed in table.

Table: Metrics for Non-functional Requirements.

Features	Measures
Speed	• Processed transaction/ second • User/event response time • Screen refresh rate
Size	• Amount of memory (KB) • Number of RAM chips.
Ease of use	• Training time • Number of help windows
Reliability	• Mean time to failure (MTTF) • Portability of unavailability • Rate of failure occurrence
Robustness	• Time to restart after failure • Percentage of events causing failure • Probability of data corruption on failure
Portability	• Percentage of target-dependent statements • Number of target systems

Requirements which are derived from the application domain of the system instead from the needs of the users are known as domain requirements. These requirements may be new functional requirements or specify a method to perform some particular computations. In addition, these requirements include any constraint that may be present in the existing functional requirements. As domain requirements reflect the fundamentals of the application domain, it is important to understand these requirements. Also, if these requirements are not fulfilled, it may be difficult to make the system work as desired.

A system can include a number of domain requirements. For example, it may comprise a design constraint that describes the user interface, which is capable of accessing all the databases used in a system. It is important for a development team to create databases and interface designs as per established standards. Similarly, the requirements of the user such as copyright restrictions and security mechanism for the files and documents used in the system are also domain requirements. When domain requirements are not expressed clearly, it can result in the following difficulties.

- Problem of understandability: When domain requirements are specified in the language of application domain (such as mathematical expressions), it becomes difficult for software engineers to understand them.

- Problem of implicitness: When domain experts understand the domain requirements but do not express these requirements clearly, it may create a problem (due to incomplete information) for the development team to understand and implement the requirements in the system.

Requirements Engineering Process

This process is a series of activities that are performed in the requirements phase to express requirements in the Software Requirements Specification (SRS) document. It focuses on understanding the requirements and its type so that an appropriate technique is determined to carry out the Requirements Engineering (RE) process. The new software developed after collecting requirements either replaces the existing software or enhances its features and functionality. For example, the payment mode of the existing software can be changed from payment through hand-written cheques to electronic payment of bills.

An RE process is shown, which comprises various steps including feasibility study, requirements elicitation, requirements analysis, requirements specification, requirements validation, and requirements management.

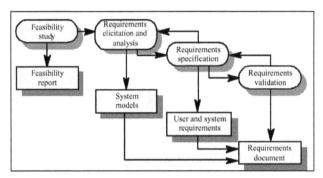

The requirements engineering process begins with feasibility study of the requirements. Then requirements elicitation is performed, which focuses on gathering user requirements. After the requirements are gathered, an analysis is performed, which further leads to requirements specification. The output of this is stored in the form of software requirements specification document. Next, the requirements are checked for their completeness and correctness in requirements validation. Last of all, to understand and control changes to system requirements, requirements management is performed.

Functional Requirement

A requirement is a description of the service that software must offer. A requirement can range from the high-level abstract statement of the sender's necessity to detailed mathematical functional requirement specifications.

In software engineering, a functional requirement defines a system or its component. It describes the functions software must perform. A function is nothing but inputs, its behavior, and outputs. It can be a calculation, data manipulation, business process, user interaction, or any other specific functionality which defines what function a system is likely to perform. Functional Requirements are also called Functional Specification.

Functional software requirements help you to capture the intended behavior of the system. This behavior may be expressed as functions, services or tasks or which system is required to perform.

What Should be Included in the Functional Requirements Document?

Table: Example Functional Requirements.

Function Requirement No.	Function Requirement Description
FR 1	User should be able to enter sales data.
FR 2	Sales report should be generated every 24 hours.
FR 3	API interface to invoice system.

Functional Requirements should include the following things:

- Details of operations conducted in every screen.
- Data handling logic should be entered into the system.
- It should have descriptions of system reports or other outputs.
- Complete information about the workflows performed by the system.
- It should clearly define who will be allowed to create/modify/delete the data in the system.
- How the system will fulfill applicable regulatory and compliance needs should be captured in the functional document.

Benefits of Functional Requirement

Here, are the pros/advantages of creating a typical functional requirement document:

- Helps you to check whether the application is providing all the functionalities that were mentioned in the functional requirement of that application.
- A functional requirement document helps you to define the functionality of a system or one of its subsystems.
- Functional requirements along with requirement analysis help identify missing requirements. They help clearly define the expected system service and behavior.
- Errors caught in the Functional requirement gathering stage are the cheapest to fix.
- Support user goals, tasks, or activities.

Types of Functional Requirements

Here, are the most common functional requirement types:

- Transaction Handling
- Business Rules
- Certification Requirements
- Reporting Requirements
- Administrative functions
- Authorization levels
- Audit Tracking
- External Interfaces
- Historical Data management
- Legal and Regulatory Requirements

Example of Functional Requirements

- The software automatically validates customers against the ABC Contact Management System.

- The Sales system should allow users to record customer's sales.

- The background color for all windows in the application will be blue and have a hexadecimal RGB color value of 0x0000FF.

- Only Managerial level employees have the right to view revenue data.

- The software system should be integrated with banking API.

Non-functional vs. Functional Requirements

Here, are key differences between Functional and Non-functional Requirements:

Parameters	Functional Requirement	Non-Functional Requirement
What it is	Verb	Attributes
Requirement	It is mandatory	It is non-mandatory
Capturing type	It is captured in use case.	It is captured as a quality attribute.
End result	Product feature	Product properties
Capturing	Easy to capture	Hard to capture
Objective	Helps you verify the functionality of the software.	Helps you to verify the performance of the software.
Area of focus	Focus on user requirement	Concentrates on the user's expectation.
Documentation	Describe what the product does	Describes how the product works
Type of Testing	Functional Testing like System, Integration, End to End, API testing, etc.	Non-Functional Testing like Performance, Stress, Usability, Security testing, etc.
Test Execution	Test Execution is done before non-functional testing.	After the functional testing
Product Info	Product Features	Product Properties

Best Practice of Functional Requirement

Important best practice for developing functional requirement document is as follows:

- Do not combine two requirements into one. Keep the requirements granular.

- You should make each requirement as complete and accurate as possible.

- The document should draft all the technical requirements.

- Map all requirements to the objectives and principles which contributes to successful software delivery.

- Elicit requirements using interviews, workshops and casual communications.

- If there is any known, verified constraint which materially affects a requirement then it is a critical state that should be documented.

- It is necessary that you document all the assumption in the document.

Mistakes While Creating a Functional Requirement

Here, are some common mistakes made while creating function requirement document:

- Putting in unjustified extra information that may confuse developers.

- Not putting sufficient detail in the requirement document.

- You add rules or examples, scoping statements or objectives anything except the requirement itself.

- Left out a piece of important information that is an absolute must to fully, accurately, and definitively state the requirement.

- Some professionals start to defend the requirements they have documented when the requirement is modified, instead of finding the correct truth.

- Requirements which are not mapped to an objective or principle.

Non-functional Requirement

A Non-Functional Requirement (NFR) defines the quality attribute of a software system. They represent a set of standards used to judge the specific operation of a system. Example, how fast does the website load.

A non-functional requirement is essential to ensure the usability and effectiveness of the entire software system. Failing to meet non-functional requirements can result in systems that fail to satisfy user needs.

Non-functional Requirements allows you to impose constraints or restrictions on the design of the system across the various agile backlogs. Example, the site should load in 3 seconds when the numbers of simultaneous users are > 10000. Description of non-functional requirements is just as critical as a functional requirement.

Types of Non-functional Requirement

- Usability requirement

- Serviceability requirement

- Manageability requirement

- Recoverability requirement

- Security requirement

- Data Integrity requirement

- Capacity requirement

- Availability requirement

- Scalability requirement

- Interoperability requirement

- Reliability requirement

- Maintainability requirement

- Regulatory requirement

- Environmental requirement

Examples of Non-functional Requirements

Here, are some examples of non-functional requirement:

- Users must change the initially assigned login password immediately after the first successful login. Moreover, the initial should never be reused.

- Employees never allowed updating their salary information. Such attempt should be reported to the security administrator.

- Every unsuccessful attempt by a user to access an item of data shall be recorded on an audit trail.

- A website should be capable enough to handle 20 million users with affecting its performance.

- The software should be portable. So moving from one OS to other OS does not create any problem.

- Privacy of information, the export of restricted technologies, intellectual property rights, etc. should be audited.

Functional vs. Non Functional Requirements

Parameters	Functional Requirement	Non-Functional Requirement
What is it?	Verb	Attributes
Requirement	It is mandatory	It is non-mandatory
Capturing type	It is captured in use case.	It is captured as a quality attribute.
End-result	Product feature	Product properties
Capturing	Easy to capture	Hard to capture
Objective	Helps you verify the functionality of the software.	Helps you to verify the performance of the software.
Area of focus	Focus on user requirement	Concentrates on the user's expectation.
Documentation	Describe what the product does	Describes how the product works
Type of Testing	Functional Testing like System, Integration, End to End, API testing, etc.	Non-Functional Testing like Performance, Stress, Usability, Security testing, etc.
Test Execution	Test Execution is done before non-functional testing.	After the functional testing
Product Info	Product Features	Product Properties

Advantages of Non-Functional Requirement

Benefits/pros of Non-functional testing are:

- The non-functional requirements ensure the software system follow legal and compliance rules.

- They ensure the reliability, availability, and performance of the software system.

- They ensure good user experience and ease of operating the software.

- They help in formulating security policy of the software system.

Disadvantages of Non-functional Requirement

Cons/drawbacks of Non-function requirement are:

- None functional requirement may affect the various high-level software subsystem.

- They require special consideration during the software architecture/high-level design phase which increases costs.

- Their implementation does not usually map to the specific software sub-system.

- It is tough to modify non-functional once you pass the architecture phase.

Summary:

- A non-functional requirement defines the performance attribute of a software system.

- Types of Non-functional requirement are Scalability Capacity, Availability, Reliability, Recoverability, Data Integrity, etc.

- Example of Non Functional Requirement is Employees never allowed to update their salary information. Such attempt should be reported to the security administrator.

- Functional Requirement is a verb while Non-Functional Requirement is an attribute.

- The advantage of Non-functional requirement is that it helps you to ensure good user experience and ease of operating the software.

- The biggest disadvantage of Non-functional requirement is that it may affect the various high-level software subsystems.

Software Requirement Life Cycle

SDLC is a process which defines the various stages involved in the development of software for delivering a high-quality product. SDLC stages cover the complete life cycle of software i.e. from inception to retirement of the product. Adhering to the SDLC process leads to the development of the software in a systematic and disciplined manner.

Purpose

Purpose of SDLC is to deliver a high-quality product which is as per the customer's requirement.

SDLC has defined its phases as, Requirement gathering, Designing, Coding, Testing, and Maintenance. It is important to adhere to the phases to provide the Product in a systematic manner.

For Example: Software has to be developed and a team is divided to work on a feature of the product and is allowed to work as they want. One of the developers decides to design first whereas the other decides to code first and the other on the documentation part.

This will lead to project failure because of which it is necessary to have a good knowledge and understanding among the team members to deliver an expected product.

SDLC Cycle

SDLC Cycle represents the process of developing software.

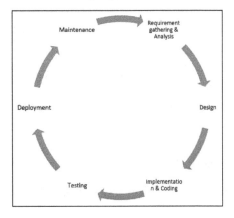

SDLC Cycle

SDLC Phases

Given below are the various phases:

- Requirement gathering and analysis
- Design
- Implementation or coding
- Testing
- Deployment
- Maintenance

Requirement Gathering and Analysis

During this phase, all the relevant information is collected from the customer to develop a product as per their expectation. Any ambiguities must be resolved in this phase only.

Business analyst and Project Manager set up a meeting with the customer to gather all the information like what the customer wants to build, who will be the end-user, what is the purpose of the product. Before building a product a core understanding or knowledge of the product is very important.

For Example: A customer wants to have an application which involves money transactions. In this case, the requirement has to be clear like what kind of transactions will be done, how it will be done, in which currency it will be done, etc.

Once the requirement gathering is done, an analysis is done to check the feasibility of the development of a product. In case of any ambiguity, a call is set up for further discussion.

Once the requirement is clearly understood, the SRS (Software Requirement Specification) document is created. This document should be thoroughly understood by the developers and also should be reviewed by the customer for future reference.

Design

In this phase, the requirement gathered in the SRS document is used as an input and software architecture that is used for implementing system development is derived.

Implementation or Coding

Implementation/Coding starts once the developer gets the Design document. The Software design is translated into source code. All the components of the software are implemented in this phase.

Testing

Testing starts once the coding is complete and the modules are released for testing. In this phase, the developed software is tested thoroughly and any defects found are assigned to developers to get them fixed.

Retesting, regression testing is done until the point at which the software is as per the customer's expectation. Testers refer SRS document to make sure that the software is as per the customer's standard.

Deployment

Once the product is tested, it is deployed in the production environment or first UAT (User Acceptance testing) is done depending on the customer expectation.

In the case of UAT, a replica of the production environment is created and the customer along with the developers does the testing. If the customer finds the application as expected, then sign off is provided by the customer to go live.

Maintenance

After the deployment of a product on the production environment, maintenance of the product i.e. if any issue comes up and needs to be fixed or any enhancement is to be done is taken care by the developers.

Requirement Analysis

Consider example of an educational software system where a student can register for different courses.

Let's study how to analyze the requirements. The requirements must maintain a standard quality of its requirement, different types of requirement quality includes:

- Atomic

- Uniquely identified

- Complete

- Consistent and unambiguous

- Traceable

- Prioritized

- Testable

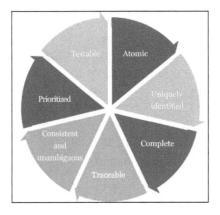

Let understand this with an example, there are three columns in the table shown here:

- The first column indicates- "requirement quality".

- The second column indicates- "bad requirement with some problem".

- The third column is same as second column but – "converted into a good requirement".

Requirement Quality	Example of bad requirement	Example of good requirement
Atomic	Students will be able to enroll to undergraduate and post graduate courses.	Students will be able to enroll to undergraduate courses. Students will be able to enroll to post-graduate courses.
Uniquely identified	1- Students will be able to enroll to undergraduate courses 1- Students will be able to enroll to post-graduate courses.	Course Enrolment. Students will be able to enroll to undergraduate courses. Students will be able to enroll to post-graduate courses.

Complete	A professor user will log into the system by providing his username, password, and other relevant information.	A professor user will log into the system by providing his username, password and department code.
Consistent and unambiguous	A student will have either undergraduate courses or post-graduate courses but not both. Some courses will be open to both under-graduate and post-graduate.	A student will have either under-graduate or post graduates but not both.
Traceable	Maintain student information-mapped to BRD req.ID?	Maintain student information-Mapped to BRD req ID 4.1.
Prioritized	Registered student-Priority: 1. Maintain User Information-Priority 1. Enroll courses-Priority 1. View Report Card-Priority 1.	Register Student-Priority: 1. Maintain User Information-Priority 2. Enroll courses-Priority 3.View Report Card-Priority.
Testable	Each page of the system will load in an acceptable time-frame.	Register student and enrol courses pages of the system will load within 5 seconds.

Now let's understand each of these requirements in details starting with Atomic.

Atomic

Atomic	1. Student will be able to enroll to undergraduate and post graduate courses.	1. Student will be able to enroll to under- graduate courses. 2. Student will be able to enroll to post- graduate courses.

So each and every requirement you have should be atomic, which means it should be at very low level of details it should not be possible to separated out into components. Here we will see the two examples for requirements, at Atomic and uniquely identified requirements levels.

So let us continue with example of system build for education domain. Here, the bad requirement is "Students will be able to enroll to undergraduate and post graduate courses" . This is a bad requirement because it is not atomic because it talks about two different entities undergraduates and post-graduates courses. So obviously it is not a good requirement but bad requirement, so correspondence good requirement would be to separate it out into two requirements. So one talks about the enrolment to undergraduate courses while the other talks about the enrolment to the post-graduate courses.

Uniquely Identified

Uniquely Identified	1- Student will be able to enroll to un- der- graduate courses. 1- Student will be able to enroll to post- graduate courses.	1- Course enrolment 1.1- Student will be able to enroll to under- graduate courses. 1.2- Student will be able to enroll to post- graduate courses.

Similarly the next requirement quality is to check for uniquely identified, here we have two separate requirement but they both have same ID#1. So, if we are referring our requirement with reference to ID#, but it is not clear which exact requirement we are referring to document or other parts of the system as both have same ID#1. So separating out with unique id's, so good requirement will be re-return as section 1- course enrolments, and it has two requirements 1.1 id is enrolment to undergraduate courses while 1.2 id is enrolment to postgraduate courses.

Complete

Complete	A professor user will log into the system by providing his username password, and other relevant information.	A professor user will log into the system by providing his username password, and department code.

Also, each and every requirement should be complete. For example, here the bad requirement says a "professor user will log into the system by providing his username, password and other relevant information". Here the other relevant information is not clear, so the other relevant information should be spelt out in good requirement to make the requirement complete.

Consistent and Unambiguous

Consistent and unambiguous	A student will have either undergraduate courses but not both.	A student will have either under-graduate or post graduate but not both.
	Some courses will be open to both under-graduate and post- graduate.	

Next each and every requirement should be consistent and unambiguous, so here for instance we have requirements "A student will have either undergraduate courses or post-graduate courses but not both" this is one requirement there is some other requirement that says "Some courses will be open to both under-graduate and post-graduate students".

The problem in this requirement is that from the first requirement it seems that the courses are divided into two categories under graduate courses and post graduate courses and student can opt either of two but not both. But when you read other requirement it conflicts with the first requirement and it tells that some courses will open to both post-graduate and under-graduate.

So it is obvious to convert this bad requirement into good requirement which is "A student will have either under-graduate courses or post-graduate courses but not both". This means that every course will be marked either being as under-graduate course or post-graduate course.

Traceable

Traceable	Maintain student information – mapped to BRD req. id?	Maintain student information – mapped to BRD req. id 4.1

Each and every requirement should be traceable because there are already different levels of requirement, we already saw that at the top we had business requirements, and then we have an architectural and design requirements followed by system integration requirements.

Now when we convert business requirement into architectural and design requirements or we convert architectural and design requirements to system integration requirements there has to be traceability. Which means that we should be able to take each and every business requirements and map it to the corresponding one or more software architectural and design requirement. So here is an example of bad requirement that says "Maintain student information – mapped to BRD req ID?" the requirement id is not given over here.

So, converting it to a good requirement it says same thing but it is mapped with the requirement id 4.1. So mapping should be there for each and every requirement. Same way we have high level and low level mapping requirement, the mapping is also there between system and integration requirement to the code that implements that requirement and also there is a mapping between the system and integration requirement to the test case which test that particular requirement.

So, this traceability is all across entire project.

Prioritized

Prioritized	Registered student-Priority 1	Register Student-Priority 1
	Maintain User Information-Priority 1	Maintain User Information-Priority 2
	Enroll courses-Priority 1	Enroll courses-Priority 1
	View Report Card-Priority 1	View Report Card-Priority3

Then each and every requirement must be prioritized, so the team has guideline so which requirement that able to implement first and which can be done later on. Here you can see the bad priority has register student, maintain user information and each and every requirement has given priority-1. Everything cannot be at same priority, so requirement can be prioritized. So the example of good requirement over here is the register student and enroll courses is given the highest priority 1, while maintain user information comes below at priority 2 and then we have view report card at priority-3.

Testable

Testable	Each page of the system will load in an acceptable time-frame.	Register student and enrol courses pages of the system will load within 5 seconds.

Each and every requirement should be testable; here the bad requirement is "each page of the system will load in an acceptable time frame". Now there are two problems with this requirement first is that each page meaning that there can be many pages, which going to blow up the testing efforts. The other problem is that it says the page is going to load in acceptable time frame, now what is acceptable time frame? Acceptable to whom. So we have to convert the non-testable argument into a testable argument, which specifically tells about which page we are talking about "register student and enroll courses pages" and the acceptable time frame is also given which is 5 seconds.

References

- Softwarerequirement: ecomputernotes.com, Retrieved 14 July, 2019
- Functional-requirement-specification-example: guru99.com, Retrieved 5 April, 2019
- Non-functional-requirement-type-example: guru99.com, Retrieved 20 February, 2019
- Software-development-life-cycle-sdlc: softwaretestinghelp.com, Retrieved 12 June, 2019
- Learn-software-requirements-analysis-with-case-study: guru99.com, Retrieved 11 January, 2019

Software Architecture

The domain of computer science which deals with the creation of the fundamental structures of a software system is known as software architecture. This chapter has been carefully written to provide an easy understanding of the varied facets of computer architecture as well as the different types of architectural design patterns.

Software Architecture also called High Level Software Design is the first design step after analyzing all requirements for software. The goal is to define a software structure which is able to fullfill the requirements. Also the non-functional requirements, such as scalability, portability and maintainability have to be considered in this step.

This first design step could be more or less independent of a programming language. However, the programming language has to be defined prior to defining the interfaces.

The Static Architecture

The first step in designing software is to define the static architecture. Simply speaking this is a very high level outline of the components and layers of software. Even if there are no requirements which explicitly ask for some of the below listed features, it is good design style to adhere to the following principles:

1. Define layers which make the functional part of the software independent of a hardware platform. There should be a hardware abstraction layer which encapsulates microcontroller specific code and features within the layer. All other layers have to be free of controller specific code. Another layer called "Physical Layer" should adapt the functional software to the specific signals. This is a data processing layer which filters signals and prepares them to be presented in physical units and defined resolutions at its interface.

2. If necessary, design a layer to adapt to a special operating system. Operating systems may offer services and semaphores, but never use them directly in your functional software. Define your own services and semaphores and go through a special layer to adapt them to the operating system services.

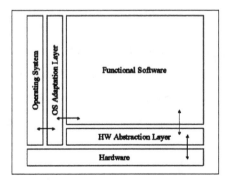

3. Design any additional layers inside your functional software as appropriate.

4. Design components inside your functional software. Depending on your requirements and future strategies it may be wise to e.g. design communication protocol components in a way that they can be easily removed and replaced by another protocol, to adapt to different platforms and systems. E.g. in the automotive industry the CAN bus is widely used for communication between the various electronic systems in a vehicle. However some customers require different communication systems as for example FlexRay or any proprietary system. Your software can be designed in a way to modify the communication systems and protocols easily. Almost as easy as "plug and play", if the design is done properly.

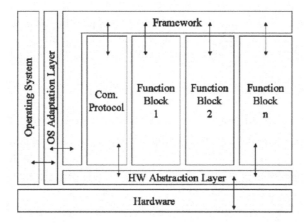

5. Design an own framework which controls the calls and interactions of your software.

6. Consider organizational aspects in your architecture. Parts of the software may be developed by different departments or even outsourced to external companies. Your static architecture has to reflect this so that complete components or even layers can be assigned to a vendor. This has to be also reflected in the interface definition.

The Interfaces

The design of your interfaces is another element which adds to the stability, portability and maintainability of your software. The following things have to be observed:

1. Only use function calls as interfaces and refrain from using memory pools or any other globally shared elements as interface.

2. Make your interfaces as narrow as possible. Therefore use simple basic data types rather than complicated proprietary structures at the interfaces. It is sometimes amazing how simple interfaces can be if the functionality is distributed in a sensible way in appropriate components.

3. Preferably make your interfaces unidirectional. This means that input components provide interfaces used by the processing components and layers. Avoid bidirectional interaction between the same components.

4.   Describe your interfaces clearly. Already in the architecture the kind of information, the data width, resolution and sign has to be defined. This is especially important if components are developed by different vendors.

The Dynamic Architecture

Operating Systems and Timing

Basically there are two categories of microcontroller systems. The first one is EVENT driven, as e.g. cell phones and other modern communication equipment.

The other kind of application is TIME driven. These microcontroller systems usually have the task to measure and evaluate signals and react on this information accordingly. This measuring activity means that signal sampling has to be performed. Additionally there may be activities like feedback current controls which have to be performed. Both activities imply by the underlying theories that sample rates have to be as exact as possible.

Both categories of systems are called realtime systems, but they are like two different worlds.

The EVENT driven systems are comparatively simple. They are usually in an idle state until one of the defined events triggers a task or process, which is executed sequentially until it is finished and the system returns to the idle state. During the execution of such a task these systems usually do not react on other events. This "first comes first serves" principle can be seen in a cell phone, where incoming calls are ignored after you started to dial an outgoing call.

TIME driven systems are much more complicated. Usually all possible inputs to the system have to be sampled and all outputs have to be served virtually simultaneously. This means that time slices have to be granted to the various activities and their duration has to be defined and limited to ensure the overall function of the system.

However there are some general rules which should be considered:

1.   The CPU selection should be made according to the application. There are some CPUs which support time driven application in an optimized way. E.g. it is recommendable to have sufficient interrupt levels, CAPCOM units and I/O ports which can be accessed without delays for time driven applications.

     In recent years some well-known microcontrollers which originate in the event driven world were pushed into the time driven market. The ease of development and stability of the systems suffer from this. Although the attempt was made by the CPU manufacturer to cover for that by designing suitable peripheral units, the whole situation still looks like an odd patchwork rather than a sound design.

2.   Operating systems can be event driven and non-pre-emptive for EVENT driven applications.

3.   Operating systems should be time driven and pre-emptive for TIME driven systems.

4.   Standard operating systems may fail you for high speed tasks, such as a 250 micro second cyclic tasks for feedback current controls. In this case you have to do this by timer interrupts outside of the operating system. Therefore have a close look at the OS from the shelf before you base your system on it.

How to Reduce Complexity in Software Design

Complexity Reduction

What can be done to reduce complexity, that is, to make system behavior more predictable? While some such as A. Berthoz have proposed a set of organizing principles based on biological systems for "simplexity", the means to provide complementary relationships between simplicity and complexity, Four possible approaches described to reduce complexity are: reduction, homogenization, abstraction, and transformation, each of which is described below:

Reduction

Reduction is the process of removing superfluous elements from the system, either in practice or in implementation, and limiting the context under which the system is allowed to operate and reducing the state space to something which is understood. For example, when using a subway system, most riders are interested in how to travel from point A to point B, making the necessary connections. A map, as shown in figure, provides just this amount of information, by eliminating elements that are not relevant to understanding this particular behavior. It should be noted that reductionism in this case does not eliminate structure, but rather makes the essential structure much more visible.

Reduction in context can be used when a system is moving into a regime in which its operation is not valid, such that steps are taken to move it back into a known space. For example, an integrated circuit's operation is well understood within certain temperature, voltage and frequency constraints and it is not allowed to operate outside this regime where it becomes far less predictable and perhaps chaotic. Thus, a potentially complex system is transformed into one that while being complicated is highly predictable.

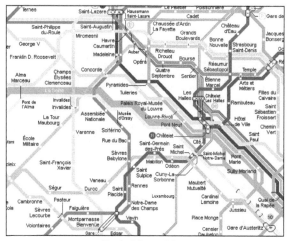

Paris Metro Map

Homogenization

Homogenization is somewhat related to reduction in that it provides the possibility to reduce the types of elements or agents by classifying them into sets that are relatively indistinguishable or homogeneous. This is the technique that allows statistics to be applied to situations rather than being forced to understand the behavior of each element. For example, it would be intractable to predict the behavior of more than a few molecules of air, yet the aggregate behavior of 10^{27} such molecules, namely pressure, volume and temperature, can be predicted with a simple ideal gas model if each molecule is treated as being indistinguishable. One should remember that if the behavior of interest is that of the individual molecules, then the system is highly unpredictable, and highly complex. Hence, the same system can be highly complex or very simple depending on the type of behavior of interest and the context of operation.

One must be very careful when applying the technique of homogenization not to overly simplify the model of the system to the point where it is not useful in predicting the desired behavior. For example, one part in a billion can make a big difference in certain reactions. In semiconductors doping levels on the order of 1 part per 100,000 can increase the conductivity of a device by a factor of 10,000 times. There are many systems in which a small amount of inhomogeneity can create starkly different behaviors. For example, pure water in isolation at 1 atmosphere pressure will freeze at -42 °C or even as low as -108 °C if cooled sufficiently quickly, while water in the presence of dust or other impurities that can serve as crystallization sites freezes at the familiar 0 °C.

Abstraction

Abstraction is essentially the ability to decouple elements in a system and transform it from a woven to a folded statement in which interactions are restricted. A good ex- ample for this part is language and thought: the more abstraction we enter in our language by encapsulating a notion into a word, the more we will be able to deal with the complexities of a conceptual problem. In fact, the creation of jargon in a scientific field is a form of abstraction that serves to reduce the complexity of that field. Mead and codified this layering, and helped to transform complexity to complication in VLSI systems. This success has allowed the creation of incredibly complicated systems with deterministic behavior which has driven software complexity and net- working which has driven us to very complex systems.

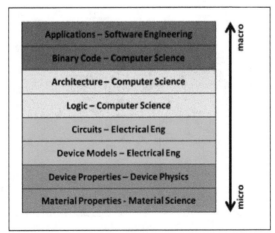

Layering within Computing Systems utilizing VLSI Technology.

It is also interesting to note that abstraction reduces the complexity at the existing boundary of a system, but it also creates a new level of complexity. In fact, this is one of the main mechanisms behind the progress of various fields in human knowledge: Efforts to reduce complexity results in creation of new level of abstractions. The resulting abstractions create a new boundary for the system and generate a new form of complexity, and the cycle continues.

Transformation

Transformation is a technique in which the problem space is altered such that it be- comes more tractable and predictable. An example of this is taking a system that is very difficult to understand in the time domain and performing analysis on it in the frequency domain. Moving from systems governed by rules to ones governed by principles may be seen as a form of transformation. Sometimes perspective can have an enormous impact on one's ability to understand a system's behavior.

One of the important studies in systems science is that of networks. In this case, the system is analyzed with a transformation of its precise structure, to one that is characterized by local and non-local connectivity and diameter (degrees of separation). This transformation enables a significant reduction in the number of factors that need to be addressed to understand the behavior of the system. Each of the systems shown in figure is composed of networks of systems that experienced evolutionary processes and as a result have a similar network structure with respect to connectivity and diameter. In this case these are composed of 'scale free' networks whose degree distribution follows a power law, such that a small number of nodes have a large number of interconnections, while most have a small number of inter- connects.

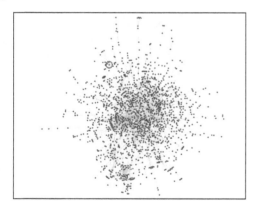 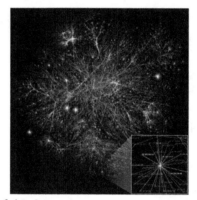

Network Structures in Evolving Systems.

It is known that these types of systems are rather resilient to random faults or at- tacks, yet are very susceptible to failure in the "too big to fail" nodes. These systems also involve tipping points which when tipped places the system in a different state such that it is usually not easy to return to the prior state. Thus, much can be under- stood about the system based on a small amount of information.

Logical Design for Software Architecture

The intended meaning of the term logical architecture often appears clear but researchers differ when it comes to the details of what it means. In the paper, Kruchten said, "The logical architecture primarily sup- ports the functional requirements – what the system should provide in terms of services to its users. The system is decomposed into a set of key abstractions, taken (mostly) from the problem domain, in the form of objects or object classes." Hofmeister et al talked about conceptual architecture rather than logical architecture in their work. But their conceptual architecture was actually closer to runtime architecture as they say, "In the conceptual view, you model your product as a collection of decomposable, interconnected conceptual components and connectors" and their components and connectors are actually runtime elements.

A logical architecture for a software system defines a collection of components and their relationships so that realizations of the components and their relationships can satisfy all the requirements of the system.

Logical architecture can be descriptive or prescriptive. Descriptive software architecture is the architecture of the existing system and prescriptive architecture is the specification of the architecture for the software system to be built. The above is the prescriptive definition of logical architecture. Here the term component means an entity that resides inside an enclosing entity and constitutes part of it. So a component can be a target for logical architecture design unless it is an atomic component, which is a component that we decide not to decompose any further. So the above definition does not prevent the design process for logical architecture from proceeding in a recursive manner.

The Goals of Logical Architecture Design

Given the notion of logical architecture as defined, what are the ultimate goals that should be pursued to have a "good" logical architecture design? The answer depends on what one regards as the most important things in architecture design. We believe that as the first architecture design stage we should abstract from less important concerns as much as possible in logical architecture design and focus only on the most important concerns. We assert that the most important concerns for logical architecture are how we can successfully build a functionally working system at all and how we can save development effort as much as possible. For the first concern, what needs to be done is to reduce the complexity of software development. This can be naturally done by decomposing the task of developing a system into more manageable tasks of developing smaller subsystems (i.e. components) and putting them together. As a general problem solving strategy, it is often referred to as the divide- and-conquer strategy. The second concern can be ad- dressed to a great extent by not duplicating work during development or by reusing what can be reused as much as possible. We call these two concerns buildability and reusability respectively and claims the following proposition.

Proposition: The goals of logical architecture design are to assure buildability and reusability.

Architecture Design Patterns

N-Tier Design Pattern

An N-Tier Application program is one that is distributed among three or more separate computers in a distributed network.

The most common form of n-tier is the 3-tier Application, and it is classified into three categories:

- User interface programming in the user's computer,
- Business logic in a more centralized computer,
- Required data in a computer that manages a database.

This architecture model provides Software Developers to create Reusable application/systems with maximum flexibility.

In N-tier, "N" refers to a number of tiers or layers are being used like – 2-tier, 3-tier or 4-tier, etc. It is also called "Multi-Tier Architecture".

The n-tier architecture is an industry-proven software architecture model. It is suitable to support enterprise level client-server applications by providing solutions to scalability, security, fault tolerance, reusability, and maintainability. It helps developers to create flexible and reusable applications.

N-Tier Architecture

A diagrammatic representation of an n-tier system depicts here – presentation, application, and database layers.

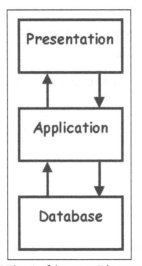

N Tier Architecture Diagram.

These three layers can be further subdivided into different sub-layers depending on the requirements.

Some common terms to remember, so as to understand the concept more clearly.

1. Distributed Network: It is a network architecture, where the components located at network computers coordinate and communicate their actions only by passing messages. It is a collection of multiple systems situated at different nodes but appears to the user as a single system.

- It provides a single data communication network which can be managed separately by different networks.

- An example of Distributed Network— where different clients are connected within LAN architecture on one side and on the other side they are connected to high-speed switches along with a rack of servers containing service nodes.

2. Client-Server Architecture: It is an architecture model where the client (one program) requests a service from a server (another program) i.e. it is a request-response service provided over the internet or through an intranet.

In this model, Client will serve as one set of program/code which executes a set of actions over the network. While Server, on the other hand, is a set of another program, which sends the result sets to the client system as requested.

- In this, client computer provides an interface to an end user to request a service or a resource from a server and on the other hand server then processes the request and displays the result to the end user.

- An example of Client-Server Model— an ATM machine. A bank is the server for processing the application within the large customer databases and ATM machine is the client having a user interface with some simple application processing.

3. Platform: In computer science or software industry, a platform is a system on which applications program can run. It consists of a combination of hardware and software that have a built-in instruction for processors/microprocessors to perform specific operations.

- In more simple words, the platform is a system or a base where any applications can run and execute to obtain a specific task.

- An example of Platform – A personal machine loaded with Windows 2000 or Mac OS X as examples of 2 different platforms.

4. Database: It is a collection of information in an organized way so that it can be easily accessed, managed and updated.

- Examples of Database – MySQL, SQL Server, and Oracle Database are some common Db's.

Types of N-Tier Architectures

There are different types of N-Tier Architectures, like 3-tier Architecture, 2-Tier Architecture and 1- Tier Architecture.

First, we will see 3-tier Architecture, which is very important.

3-Tier Architecture

By looking at the below diagram, you can easily identify that 3-tier architecture has three different layers.

- Presentation layer

- Business Logic layer

- Database layer

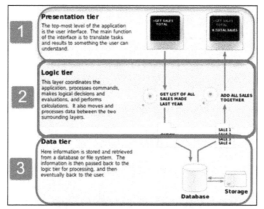

3 Tier Architecture Diagram.

Here we have taken a simple example of student form to understand all these three layers. It has information about a student like – Name, Address, Email, and Picture.

User Interface Layer or Presentation Layer

Students Information				
ID	Name	Address	Email	Picture

Presentation Layer

```
private void DataGrid1_SelectedIndexChanged(object sender, System.EventArgs e)
{
// Object of the Property layer
clsStudent objproperty=new clsStudent();
// Object of the business layer
clsStudentInfo objbs=new clsStudentInfo();
// Object of the dataset in which we receive the data sent by the business layer
DataSet ds=new DataSet();
// here we are placing the value in the property using the object of the
//property layer
objproperty.id=int.Parse(DataGrid1.SelectedItem.Cells[1].Text.ToString());


// In this following code we are calling a function from the business layer and
// passing the object of the property layer which will carry the ID till the
database.
ds=objbs.GetAllStudentBsIDWise(objproperty);
```

```
// What ever the data has been returned by the above function into the dataset
//is being populate through the presentation laye.
txtId.Text=ds.Tables[0].Rows[0][0].ToString();
txtFname.Text=ds.Tables[0].Rows[0][1].ToString();
txtAddress.Text=ds.Tables[0].Rows[0][2].ToString();
txtemail.Text=ds.Tables[0].Rows[0][3].ToString();
```

Code Explanation

- The above code defines the basic designing of a front end view of applications as well as calling of the functions of other layers so that they can be integrated with each other.

Business Access Layer

This is the function of the business layer which accepts the data from the application layer and passes it to the data layer.

- Business logic acts as an interface between Client layer and Data Access Layer.

- All business logic – like validation of data, calculations, data insertion/modification are written under business logic layer.

- It makes communication faster and easier between the client and data layer.

- Defines a proper workflow activity that is necessary to complete a task.

```
// this is the function of the business layer which accepts the data from the
//application layer and passes it to the data layer.
public class clsStudentInfo
{
        public DataSet GetAllStudentBsIDWise(clsStudent obj)
        {
          DataSet ds=new DataSet();
          ds=objdt.getdata_dtIDWise(obj);// Calling of Data layer function
          return ds;
        }
}
```

Explanation of Code

The code is using the function of business layer, which will accept the data for the application layer and passed it to the data layer. The Business layer codes act as a mediator between the functions defined in the presentation layer and data layer and calling the functions vice -versa.

Data Access Layer

This is the data layer function, which receives the data from the business layer and performs the necessary operation into the database.

```
// this is the datalayer function which is receiving the data from the business
//layer and performing the required operation into the database


public class clsStudentData // Data layer class
{
        // object of property layer class
        public DataSet getdata_dtIDUise(clsStudent obj)
        {
         DataSet ds;
         string sql;
         sql="select * from student where Studentld=" +obj.id+ "order by Studentld;
         ds=new DataSet();
        //this is the datalayer function which accepts the sql query and performs
the
        //corresponding operation
            ds=objdt.ExecuteSql(sql);
            return ds;
        }
}
```

Explanation of Code

The code defines in dataset layer above accepts the entire request: requested by the system and performing the required operations into the database.

2-Tier Architecture

It is like Client-Server architecture, where communication takes place between client and server.

In this type of software architecture, the presentation layer or user interface layer runs on the client side while dataset layer gets executed and stored on server side.

There is no Business logic layer or immediate layer in between client and server.

Single Tier or 1-Tier Architecture

It is the simplest one as it is equivalent to running the application on the personal computer. All of the required components for an application to run are on a single application or server.

Presentation layer, Business logic layer, and data layer are all located on a single machine.

Advantages and Disadvantages of Multi-Tier Architectures

Advantages	Disadvantages
• Scalability	• Increase in Effort
• Data Integrity	• Increase in Complexity
• Reusability	
• Reduced Distribution	
• Improved Security	
• Improved Availability	

Hence, it is a part of a program which encrypts real-world business problems and determines how data can be updated, created, stored, or changed to get the complete task done.

N-Tier Architecture Tips and Development

Considering the software professionals must have a full control on all the layers of the architecture, tips on n-tier architecture are given as below:

1. Try to decouple layers from another layer as much as possible by using a technique like soap XML.

2. Use some automated tools to generate a mapping between a business logic layer and a relational database layer (data layer). Tools that can help in modeling these mapping techniques are – Entity Framework and Hibernate for Net etc.

3. In client presenter layer, put a common code for all the clients in a separate library as much as possible. This will maximize the code reusability for all types of clients.

4. A cache layer can be added into an existing layer to speed up the performance.

Client–Server Architecture

Client-server architecture is architecture of a computer network in which many clients (remote processors) request and receive service from a centralized server (host computer). Client computers provide an interface to allow a computer user to request services of the server and to display the results the server returns. Servers wait for requests to arrive from clients and then respond to them. Ideally, a server provides a standardized transparent interface to clients so that clients need not be aware of the specifics of the system (i.e., the hardware and software) that is providing the service. Clients are often situated at workstations or on personal computers, while servers are located elsewhere on the network, usually on more powerful machines. This computing model is especially effective when clients and the server each have distinct tasks that they routinely perform. In hospital data processing, for example, a client computer can be running an application program for entering patient information while the server computer is running another program that manages the database in which the information is permanently stored. Many clients can access the server's information simultaneously, and, at the same time, a client computer can perform other tasks, such as sending e-mail. Because both client and server computers are considered intelligent devices, the client-server model is completely different from the old "mainframe" model, in which a centralized mainframe computer performed all the tasks for its associated "dumb" terminals.

Web-based Architecture

The web application architecture describes the interactions between applications, databases, and middleware systems on the web. It ensures that multiple applications work simultaneously. Let us understand it with a simple example of opening a webpage. As soon as the user hits the go button after typing a URL in the address bar of a web browser, it requests for that particular web address. The server sends files to the browser as a response to the request made. The browser then executes those files to show the requested page.

Finally, the user is able to interact with the website. The most important thing to note here is the code parsed by the web browser. A web app works in a similar way.

This code might or might not have specific instructions that tell the browser how to respond with respect to the different types of user inputs. Hence, web application architecture has to include all the sub-components as well as the external applications interchanges for the entire software application, in the aforementioned case, which is a website.

The web application architecture is indispensable in the modern world because a major portion of the global network traffic, as well as most of the apps and devices, make use of web-based communication. Web application architecture has to not only deal with efficiency, but also with reliability, scalability, security, and robustness.

Working

With any typical web application, there are two different codes (sub-programs) running side-by-side. These are:

- Client-side Code – The code that is in the browser and responds to some user input.

- Server-side Code – The code that is on the server and responds to the HTTP requests.

A web developer (team) developing the web application decides as to what the code on the server will do with respect to the code in the browser. For writing server-side code, C#, Java, JavaScript, Python, PHP, Ruby, etc. are used.

Any code that is able to respond to HTTP requests has the ability to run on a server. The server-side code is responsible for creating the page that the user requested as well as storing different types of data, including user profiles and user input. It is never seen by the end-user.

A combination of CSS, HTML, and JavaScript is used for writing the client-side code. This code is parsed by the web browser. Unlike the server-side code, client-side code can be seen as well as modified by the user. It reacts to user input.

The client-side code communicates only via HTTP requests and is not able to read files off a server directly.

Web Application Components

When we say web application components, we can mean any of the following two:

- UI/UX Web Application Components: This includes activity logs, dashboards, notifications, settings, statistics, etc. These components have nothing to do with the operation of a web application architecture. Instead, they are part of the interface layout plan of a web app.

- Structural Components: The two major structural components of a web app are client and server sides.

- Client Component: The client component is developed in CSS, HTML, and JS. As it exists within the user's web browser, there is no need for operating system or device-related adjustments. The client component is a representation of a web application's functionality that the end-user interacts with.

- Server Component: The server component can be build using one or a combination of several programming languages and frameworks, including Java, .Net, NodeJS, PHP, Python, and Ruby on Rails. The server component has at least two parts; app logic and database. The former is the main control center of the web application while the latter is where all the persistent data is stored.

Models of Web Application Components

Depending on the total number of servers and databases used for a web application, the model of a web app is decided. It can be any of the following three:

One Web Server, One Database

It is the most simple as well as the least reliable web app component model. Such a model uses a single server as well as a single database. A web app builds on such a model will go down as soon as the server goes down. Hence, it isn't much reliable.

One web server, one database web application component model is not typically used for real web applications. It is mostly used for running test projects as well as with the intent of learning and understanding the fundamentals of the web application.

Multiple Web Servers, One Database (At a Machine Rather than the Web server)

The idea with this type of web application component model is that the web server doesn't store any data. When the web server gets information from a client, it processes the same and then writes it to the database, which is managed outside of the server. This is sometimes also referred to as a stateless architecture.

At least 2 web servers are required for this web application component model. This is all for avoiding failure. Even when one of the web servers goes down, the other one will take charge.

All requests made will be redirected automatically to the new server and the web app will continue execution. Hence, reliability is better as compared to the single server with inherent database model. However, if the database crashes the web app will follow to do the same.

Multiple Web Server, Multiple Databases

It is the most efficient web application component model because neither the webservers nor the databases have a single point of failure. There are two options for this type of model. Either to store identical data in all the employed databases or distribute it evenly among them.

Not more than 2 databases are required typically for the former case, while for the latter case some data might become unavailable in the scenario of a database crash. DBMS normalization is used, however, in both scenarios.

When the scale is large i.e. more than 5 web servers or databases or both, it is advised to install load balancers.

Types of Web Application Architecture

Web application architecture is a pattern of interaction between various web application components. The type of web application architecture depends on how the application logic is distributed among the client and server sides.

There are three primary types of web application architecture. Each one of them is explained as follows:

Single-Page Applications (SPAs)

Instead of loading completely new pages from the server each time for a user action, single page web applications allows for a dynamic interaction by means of providing updated content to the current page.

AJAX, a concise form of Asynchronous JavaScript and XML, is the foundation for enabling page communications and hence, making SPAs a reality. Because single-page applications prevent interruptions in user experience, they, in a way, resemble traditional desktop applications.

SPAs are designed in a way so that they request for most necessary content and information elements. This leads to the procurement of an intuitive as well as interactive user experience.

Microservices

These are small and lightweight services that execute a single functionality. The Microservices Architecture framework has a number of advantages that allows developers to not only enhance productivity but also speed up the entire deployment process.

The components making up an application build using the Microservices Architecture aren't directly dependent on each other. As such, they don't necessitate to be built using the same programming language.

Hence, developers working with the Microservices Architecture are free to pick up a technology stack of choice. It makes developing the application simpler and quicker.

Serverless Architectures

In this type of web application architecture, an application developer consults a third-party cloud infrastructure services provider for outsourcing server as well as infrastructure management.

The benefit of this approach is that it allows applications to execute the code logic without bothering with the infrastructure-related tasks.

The Serverless Architecture is best when the development company doesn't want to manage or support the servers as well as the hardware they have developed the web application for.

Some Web App Development Tips

Any web application in a working state can't be labeled 'the best.' There is more than a working ability that makes a web application worthy to be called great.

In order to ensure a web application is able to give out maximum performance, a galore of points should be kept in mind during its development. The web app must:

- Avoid frequent crashes,
- Be able to scale up or down easily,
- Be simple to use,
- Have a faster response time,
- Have automated deployments,
- Log errors,
- Not have a single point of failure,
- Solve the query in a consistent and uniform manner,
- Support the latest standards and technologies,
- Utilize strengthened security measures to lessen the chance of malicious intrusions.

Web Browser

A web browser, or simply "browser," is an application used to access and view websites. Common web browsers include Microsoft Internet Explorer, Google Chrome, Mozilla Firefox, and Apple Safari.

The primary function of a web browser is to render HTML, the code used to design or "mark up" webpages. Each time a browser loads a web page, it processes the HTML, which may include text, links, and references to images and other items, such as cascading style sheets and JavaScript functions. The browser processes these items, then renders them in the browser window.

Early web browsers, such as Mosaic and Netscape Navigator, were simple applications that rendered HTML, processed form input, and supported bookmarks. As websites have evolved, so have web browser requirements. Today's browsers are far more advanced, supporting multiple types of HTML (such as XHTML and HTML 5), dynamic JavaScript, and encryption used by secure websites.

The capabilities of modern web browsers allow web developers to create highly interactive websites. For example, Ajax enables a browser to dynamically update information on a webpage without the need to reload the page. Advances in CSS allow browsers to display a responsive website layouts and a wide array of visual effects.

Web Server

A web server is server software, or hardware dedicated to running said software, that can satisfy World Wide Web client requests. A web server can, in general, contain one or more websites. A web server processes incoming network requests over HTTP and several other related protocols.

The primary function of a web server is to store, process and deliver web pages to clients. The communication between client and server takes place using the Hypertext Transfer Protocol (HTTP). Pages delivered are most frequently HTML documents, which may include images, style sheets and scripts in addition to the text content.

A user agent, commonly a web browser or web crawler, initiates communication by making a request for a specific resource using HTTP and the server responds with the content of that resource or an error message if unable to do so. The resource is typically a real file on the server's secondary storage, but this is not necessarily the case and depends on how the web server is implemented.

Multiple web servers may be used for a high traffic website; here, Dell servers are installed together being used for the Wikimedia Foundation.

While the primary function is to serve content, a full implementation of HTTP also includes ways of receiving content from clients. This feature is used for submitting web forms, including uploading of files.

Many generic web servers also support server-side scripting using Active Server Pages (ASP), PHP (Hypertext Preprocessor), or other scripting languages. This means that the behaviour of the web server can be scripted in separate files, while the actual server software remains unchanged. Usually, this function is used to generate HTML documents dynamically ("on-the-fly") as opposed to returning static documents. The former is primarily used for retrieving or modifying information from databases. The latter is typically much faster and more easily cached but cannot deliver dynamic content.

Web servers can frequently be found embedded in devices such as printers, routers, webcams and serving only a local network. The web server may then be used as a part of a system for monitoring or administering the device in question. This usually means that no additional software has to be installed on the client computer since only a web browser is required (which now is included with most operating systems).

Application Server

An application server is a type of server designed to install, operate and host applications and associated services for end users, IT services and organizations. It facilitates the hosting and delivery of high-end consumer or business applications, which are used by multiple and simultaneously connected local or remote users.

An application server consists of a server operating system (OS) and server hardware that work together to provide computing-intensive operations and services to the residing application. An application server executes and provides user and/or other app access when utilizing the installed application's business/functional logic. Key required features of an application server include data redundancy, high availability, load balancing, user management, data/application security and a centralized management interface. Moreover, an application server may be connected by enterprise systems, networks or intranet and remotely accessed via the Internet.

Depending on the installed application, an application server may be classified in a variety of ways, including as a Web server, database application server, general purpose application server or enterprise application (EA) server.

Service-Oriented Architecture

Service-Oriented Architecture (SOA) is an architectural approach in which applications make use of services available in the network. In this architecture, services are provided to form applications, through a communication call over the internet.

- SOA allows users to combine a large number of facilities from existing services to form applications.

- SOA encompasses a set of design principles that structure system development and provide means for integrating components into a coherent and decentralized system.

- SOA based computing packages functionalities into a set of interoperable services, which can be integrated into different software systems belonging to separate business domains.

There are two major roles within Service-oriented Architecture:

- Service provider: The service provider is the maintainer of the service and the organization that makes available one or more services for others to use. To advertise services, the provider can publish them in a registry, together with a service contract that specifies the nature of the service, how to use it, the requirements for the service, and the fees charged.

- Service consumer: The service consumer can locate the service metadata in the registry and develop the required client components to bind and use the service.

Services might aggregate information and data retrieved from other services or create workflows of services to satisfy the request of a given service consumer. This practice is known as service orchestration. Another important interaction pattern is service choreography, which is the coordinated interaction of services without a single point of control.

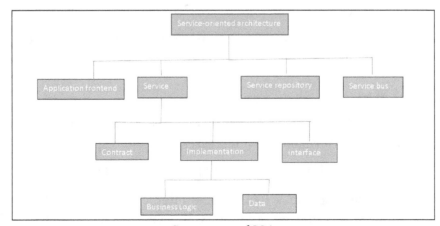

Components of SOA.

Guiding Principles of SOA

- Standardized service contract: Specified through one or more service description documents.

- Loose coupling: Services are designed as self-contained components; maintain relationships that minimize dependencies on other services.

- Abstraction: A service is completely defined by service contracts and description documents. They hide their logic, which is encapsulated within their implementation.

- Reusability: Designed as components, services can be reused more effectively, thus reducing development time and the associated costs.

- Autonomy: Services have control over the logic they encapsulate and, from a service consumer point of view; there is no need to know about their implementation.

- Discoverability: Services are defined by description documents that constitute supplemental metadata through which they can be effectively discovered. Service discovery provides an effective means for utilizing third-party resources.

- Composability: Using services as building blocks, sophisticated and complex operations can be implemented. Service orchestration and choreography provide a solid support for composing services and achieving business goals.

Advantages of SOA

- Service reusability: In SOA, applications are made from existing services. Thus, services can be reused to make many applications.

- Easy maintenance: As services are independent of each other they can be updated and modified easily without affecting other services.

- Platform independent: SOA allows making a complex application by combining services picked from different sources, independent of the platform.

- Availability: SOA facilities are easily available to anyone on request.

- Reliability: SOA applications are more reliable because it is easy to debug small services rather than huge codes.

- Scalability: Services can run on different servers within an environment, this increases scalability.

Disadvantages of SOA

- High overhead: A validation of input parameters of services is done whenever services interact this decreases performance as it increases load and response time.

- High investment: A huge initial investment is required for SOA.

- Complex service management: When services interact they exchange messages to tasks. The number of messages may go in millions. It becomes a cumbersome task to handle a large number of messages.

Practical Applications of SOA

SOA is used in many ways around us whether it is mentioned or not.

- SOA infrastructure is used by many armies and air force to deploy situational awareness systems.

- SOA is used to improve the healthcare delivery.

- Nowadays many apps are games and they use inbuilt functions to run. For example, an app might need GPS so it uses inbuilt GPS functions of the device. This is SOA in mobile solutions.

- SOA helps maintain museums a virtualized storage pool for their information and content.

References

- Design-high-level: the-software-experts.com, Retrieved 2 May, 2019

- Designing-logical-architectures-of-software-systems: researchgate.net, Retrieved 12 March, 2019

- N-tier-architecture-system-concepts-tips: guru99.com, Retrieved 20 August, 2019

- Web-application-architecture-definition-models-types-and-more: hackr.io, Retrieved 28 March, 2019

- Application-server: techopedia.com, Retrieved 8 July, 2019

- Service-oriented-architecture: geeksforgeeks.org, Retrieved 12 February, 2019

Software Design

The process which is involved in envisioning and defining software solutions to one or more sets of problems is referred to as software design. The patterns which are used to describe solutions to common problems are known as design patterns. The diverse aspects of software design as well as the different types of design patterns have been thoroughly discussed in this chapter.

Software Design Fundamentals

Software design is the technical kernel of the software engineering process.

Software design is a process through which the requirements are translated into a representation of software. Initially the representation depicts a holistic view of software. Subsequent refinement leads to a representation that is close to source code.

The software design process has technical and management aspects:

- From a project management point of view, software design is conducted in two steps:

  ○ Preliminary design: concerns the transformation of requirements into data and software architecture.

  ○ Detailed design: focuses on refinements to the architectural representation that lead to detailed data structure and algorithmic representations of software.

- From a technical point of view, software design involves the following steps:

  ○ Data design: transforms the information domain model created during the analysis into data structures that will be required to implement the software;

  ○ Architectural design: defines the relationship among major structural components of the program;

  ○ Procedural design: transforms the structural components into a procedural description of the software;

  ○ Interface design: establishes the layout and interaction mechanisms for human-machine interaction.

Fundamental Concepts

The software designer raises the following questions:

- What criteria can be used to partition the software into individual components?

- How function or data is structure detail separated from a conceptual representation of the software?

- Are there uniform criteria that define technical quality of software design?

The basic concepts of the software design process are:

- Abstraction

- Refinements

- Modularity

- Architecture

- Hierarchy

- Data structure

- Software procedures

- Information hiding

Object-Oriented vs. Procedural Design

Procedural Design

The procedural design is often understood as a software design process that uses mainly control commands such as: sequence, condition, repetition, which is applied to the predefined data. Sequences serve to achieve the processing steps in order that is essential in the specification of any algorithm.

Conditions provide facilities for achieving selected processing according to some logical statement. Repetitions serve to achieve loopings during the computation process.

These three commands are implemented as ready programming language constructs. The programming languages that provide such command constructs are called imperative programming languages.

The software design technique that relies on these constructs is called procedural design, or also structured design.

Object-Oriented Design

The Macro Design Process

The macro design process is closely related to the traditional waterfall life cycle, and serves as controlling framework for the micro process.

The basic philosophy of the macro process is that of incremental development. The macro design process tends to track the following activities.

Conceptualization

Includes establishing the core requirements to the software. The conceptualization may consist of the following activities:

- Assemble an appropriate team to develop a prototype;

- Develop a prototype;

- Evaluate the prototype.

The prototypes constructed at this stage are meant to be thrown away. Such prototypes are not to be allowed to evolve directly into a system. At this stage any programming paradigm may be used.

Analysis

The purpose of the analysis is to provide a description of a problem. The description must be complete, consistent, readable, and reviewable. The primary activities during the analysis are:

- Identify all primary function points of the system, if possible group them.

- Into clusters of functionally related behaviours; function points are the outwardly observable and testable behaviours of the system. From the perspective of the user, a function point represents some primary activity of the system in response to some event.

- For each set of function points storyboard a scenario using use-cases.

- Develop the use-case view of the system.

During the analysis we seek to model the world by classes from the vocabulary of the problem domain.

Design

The purpose of the design is to create the architecture of the system The primary activities during the design are:

- Allocate the clusters of function points to layers and partitions of the architecture;

- Perform one spin of corresponding micro design subprocesses;

- Validate the architecture by creating an executable release;

- Asses the risk of each architectural component.

After the global system construction, release planning sets. A typical order of events for this activity is as follows:

- Given the architectural components organize them in order of behaviors;

- Allocate the relevant function points to series of architectural releases; elaborate the component diagram and develop the component view of the system;

- Develop the deployment diagram and the deployment view of the system;

- Perform task planning, when the work breakdown structure is ready. A product of release planning is a formal development plan, which identifies the stream of architectural releases, team tasks, and risk assessments.

Evolution

This is essentially the process of implementing the system. The primary activities during the evolution process are:

- Assign tasks to the team to carry out this release;

- Initiate one spin of corresponding micro design subprocesses;

- Supervise the micro process by establishing appropriate reviews;

  ◦ Force closure of the micro process by making an executable release.

In practice the following kinds of changes are to be expected during the system evolution:

- Adding new classes to the system;

- Changing the implementation of a class;

- Changing the representation of a class;

- Changing the interface of a class.

Maintenance

This is the activity of managing postdelivery evolution of the system. The primary activities during the maintenance are:

- Prioritize the requests for major enhancement or bug reports that denote systematic problems, and asses the cost of development;

- Establish a meaningful collection of these changes and treat them as function points for next elaboration;

- If resources allow it, add more localized enhancements to the next release;

- Manage the next evolutionary release.

The Micro Design Process

The micro design process is closely related to the spiral model of software development, and serves as framework for iterative and incremental approach to development.

Identifying Classes and Objects

The purpose is to establish the boundaries of the problem.

The activities at this process are:

- Apply the classical approach to object-oriented development to generate a set of candidate classes and objects. The abstractions should be directly related to the function points.

- Develop class and object diagrams! For each abstraction do the following:

  ○ Enumerate its roles and responsibilities;

  ○ Devise a sufficient set of operations that satisfy these responsibilities;

  ○ Consider each operation in turn and ensure that it is primitive. If not, isolate and expose its more primitive operations;

  ○ Consider the needs for construction, destruction and copying;

  ○ Consider the need for completeness: add other primitive operations that are not necessarily required by the immediate clients, and would probably be used by future clients.

Identifying the Semantics of Classes and Objects

The purpose is to establish the behavior and attributes of each abstraction. Here we refine the abstractions through distribution of the responsibilities.

A typical order of events might be the following:

- Create a scenario or scenarios related to a single function point,

- Walk through the activities of the scenarios, assigning responsibilities to each abstraction sufficient to accomplish the desired behavior. If necessary, assign attributes that represent structural elements required to carry out certain responsibilities,

- Reallocate responsibilities so that there is a reasonably balanced distribution of behavior. Where possible reuse or adapt existing responsibilities. Splitting large responsibilities to smaller ones is very common action,

- Elaborate the state diagrams and sequence diagrams.

Identifying the Relationships Among Classes and Objects

The purpose is to solidify the boundaries of and to recognize the collaborations with each abstraction. This activity formalizes the conceptual as well as physical separations of concern among the abstractions.

The activities night is:

- Collect a set of classes at a given level of abstraction and add the significant properties relevant to the problem being modeled;

- Establish association relationships in case of presented semantic dependencies; some associations may immediately be identified as specialization/generalization or aggregation relationships;

- For each association specify the role of each participant, as well as any relevant cardinality or other kind of constraint;

- Validate the decisions by walk through scenarios;

- Develop collaboration diagrams.

Inheritance, containment, instantiation and use are the main kinds of relationships of interest, together with other properties as labels, cardinality, and so on:

- Given a collection of classes clustered by some set of associations, look for patterns of behavior that represents opportunities for specialization/generalization. Place the classes in context of the inheritance lattice, or fabricate another one;

- If there are patterns of structure, consider creating new classes that capture this common structure, and introduce them either through inheritance or through aggregation;

- As development proceeds, introduce tactical details such as: roles, keys, cardinalities, friendship, and so on.

Implementing Classes and Objects

The purpose is to provide a refinement of the existing abstractions, sufficient to unveil new classes and objects at the next level of abstraction, which we feed at the next iteration. A typical order of events may be the following:

- For each class consider its protocol. Determine which operations need to be optimized. Develop precise signatures for all significant operations;

- Adjust the inheritance lattice if required;

- Alter local implementations of abstractions that are not time or space efficient;

- Check whether the algorithms for the operations are suitable.

Component Diagrams

Component diagrams are used in modeling the physical aspects of object-oriented systems that are used for visualizing, specifying, and documenting component-based systems and also for constructing executable systems through forward and reverse engineering. Component diagrams are essentially class diagrams that focus on a system's components that often used to model the static implementation view of a system.

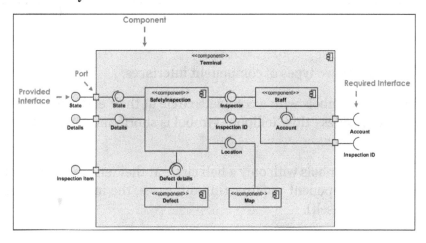

A component diagram breaks down the actual system under development into various high levels of functionality. Each component is responsible for one clear aim within the entire system and only interacts with other essential elements on a need-to-know basis.

The example above shows the internal components of a larger component:

- The data (account and inspection ID) flows into the component via the port on the right-hand side and is converted into a format the internal components can use. The interfaces on the right are known as required interfaces, which represents the services the component needed in order to carry out its duty.

- The data then passes to and through several other components via various connections before it is output at the ports on the left. Those interfaces on the left are known as provided interface, which represents the services to deliver by the exhibiting component.

- It is important to note that the internal components are surrounded by a large 'box' which can be the overall system itself (in which case there would not be a component symbol in the top right corner) or a subsystem or component of the overall system (in this case the 'box' is a component itself).

Basic Concepts of Component Diagram

A component represents a modular part of a system that encapsulates its contents and whose manifestation is replaceable within its environment. In UML 2, a component is drawn as a rectangle with optional compartments stacked vertically. A high-level, abstracted view of a component in UML 2 can be modelled as:

- A rectangle with the component's name

- A rectangle with the component icon

- A rectangle with the stereotype text and/or icon

Interface

In the example below shows two types of component interfaces:

- Provided interface symbols with a complete circle at their end represent an interface that the component provides - this "lollipop" symbol is shorthand for a realization relationship of an interface classifier.

- Required Interface symbols with only a half circle at their end (a.k.a. sockets) represent an interface that the component requires (in both cases, the interface's name is placed near the interface symbol itself).

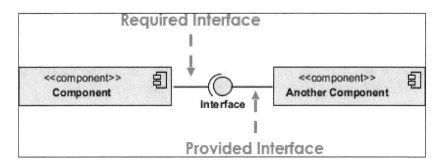

Component Diagram Example - Using Interface (Order System)

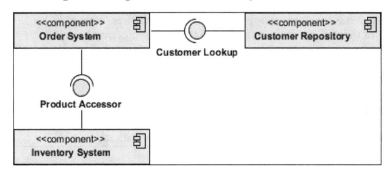

Subsystems

The subsystem classifier is a specialized version of a component classifier. Because of this, the subsystem notation element inherits all the same rules as the component notation element. The only difference is that a subsystem notation element has the keyword of subsystem instead of component.

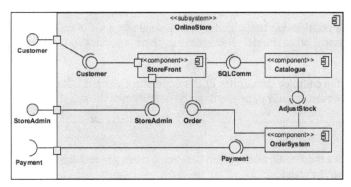

Port

Ports are represented using a square along the edge of the system or a component. A port is often used to help expose required and provided interfaces of a component.

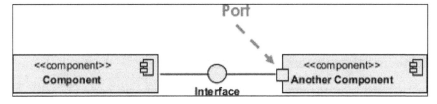

Relationships

Graphically, a component diagram is a collection of vertices and arcs and commonly contains components, interfaces and dependency, aggregation, constraint, generalization, association, and realization relationships. It may also contain notes and constraints.

Relationships	Notation
Association • An association specifies a semantic relationship that can occur between typed instances. • It has at least two ends represented by properties, each of which is connected to the type of the end. More than one end of the association may have the same type.	
Composition • Composite aggregation is a strong form of aggregation that requires a part instance be included in at most one composite at a time. • If a composite is deleted, all of its parts are normally deleted with it.	
Aggregation • A kind of association that has one of its end marked shared as kind of aggregation, meaning that it has a shared aggregation.	
Constraint • A condition or restriction expressed in natural language text or in a machine readable language for the purpose of declaring some of the semantics of an element.	
Dependency • A dependency is a relationship that signifies that a single or a set of model elements requires other model elements for their specification or implementation. • This means that the complete semantics of the depending elements is either semantically or structurally dependent on the definition of the supplier element(s).	
Links • A generalization is a taxonomic relationship between a more general classifier and a more specific classifier. • Each instance of the specific classifier is also an indirect instance of the general classifier. • Thus, the specific classifier inherits the features of the more general classifier.	

Modeling Source Code

- Either by forward or reverse engineering identifies the set of source code files of interest and model them as components stereotyped as files.

- For larger systems, use packages to show groups of source code files.

- Consider exposing a tagged value indicating such information as the version number of the source code file, its author, and the date it was last changed. Use tools to manage the value of this tag.

- Model the compilation dependencies among these files using dependencies. Again, use tools to help generate and manage these dependencies.

Component Example - Java Source Code

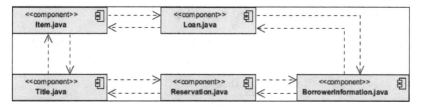

Component Diagram Example - C++ Code with versioning

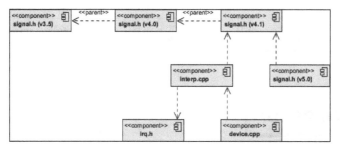

Modeling an Executable Release

- Identify the set of components you'd like to model. Typically, this will involve some or all the components that live on one node or the distribution of these sets of components across all the nodes in the system.

- Consider the stereotype of each component in this set. For most systems, you'll find a small number of different kinds of components (such as executables, libraries, tables, files, and documents). You can use the UML's extensibility mechanisms to provide visual cues (clues) for these stereotypes.

- For each component in this set, consider its relationship to its neighbors. Most often, this will involve interfaces that are exported (realized) by certain components and then imported (used) by others. If you want to expose the seams in your system, model these interfaces explicitly. If you want your model at a higher level of abstraction, elide these relationships by showing only dependencies among the components.

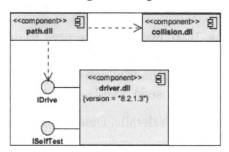

Modeling a Physical Database

- Identify the classes in your model that represent your logical database schema.

- Select a strategy for mapping these classes to tables. You will also want to consider the physical distribution of your databases. Your mapping strategy will be affected by the location in which you want your data to live on your deployed system.

- To visualize, specify, construct, and document your mapping, create a component diagram that contains components stereotyped as tables.

- Where possible, use tools to help you transform your logical design into a physical design.

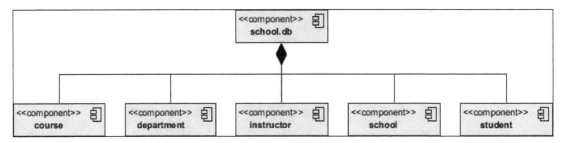

Data Flow Diagram

A Data Flow Diagram (DFD) is a traditional visual representation of the information flows within a system. A neat and clear DFD can depict the right amount of the system requirement graphically. It can be manual, automated, or a combination of both.

It shows how data enters and leaves the system, what changes the information, and where data is stored.

The objective of a DFD is to show the scope and boundaries of a system as a whole. It may be used as a communication tool between a system analyst and any person who plays a part in the order that acts as a starting point for redesigning a system. The DFD is also called as a data flow graph or bubble chart.

The following observations about DFDs are essential:

1. All names should be unique. This makes it easier to refer to elements in the DFD.

2. Remember that DFD is not a flow chart. Arrows is a flow chart that represents the order of events; arrows in DFD represents flowing data. A DFD does not involve any order of events.

3. Suppress logical decisions. If we ever have the urge to draw a diamond-shaped box in a DFD, suppress that urge! A diamond-shaped box is used in flow charts to represents decision points with multiple exists paths of which the only one is taken. This implies an ordering of events, which makes no sense in a DFD.

4. Do not become bogged down with details. Defer error conditions and error handling until the end of the analysis.

Standard symbols for DFDs are derived from the electric circuit diagram analysis and are shown in figure:

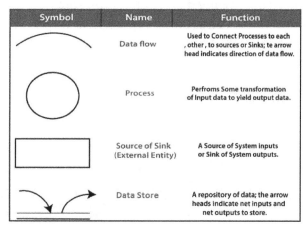

Symbol	Name	Function
	Data flow	Used to Connect Processes to each, other, to sources or Sinks; te arrow head indicates direction of data flow.
	Process	Perfroms Some transformation of Input data to yield output data.
	Source of Sink (External Entity)	A Source of System inputs or Sink of System outputs.
	Data Store	A repository of data; the arrow heads indicate net inputs and net outputs to store.

Symbols for Data Flow Diagrams.

- Circle: A circle (bubble) shows a process that transforms data inputs into data outputs.

- Data Flow: A curved line shows the flow of data into or out of a process or data store.

- Data Store: A set of parallel lines shows a place for the collection of data items. A data store indicates that the data is stored which can be used at a later stage or by the other processes in a different order. The data store can have an element or group of elements.

- Source or Sink: Source or Sink is an external entity and acts as a source of system inputs or sink of system outputs.

Levels in Data Flow Diagrams (DFD)

The DFD may be used to perform a system or software at any level of abstraction. Infact, DFDs may be partitioned into levels that represent increasing information flow and functional detail. Levels in DFD are numbered 0, 1, 2 or beyond. Here, we will see primarily three levels in the data flow diagram, which are: 0-level DFD, 1-level DFD, and 2-level DFD.

0-level DFDM

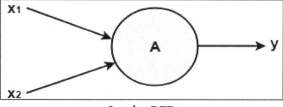

Level-0 DFD

It is also known as fundamental system model, or context diagram represents the entire software requirement as a single bubble with input and output data denoted by incoming and outgoing arrows. Then the system is decomposed and described as a DFD with multiple bubbles. Parts of the system represented by each of these bubbles are then decomposed and documented as more and more detailed DFDs. This process may be repeated at as many levels as necessary until the program at hand is well understood. It is essential to preserve the number of inputs and outputs between levels, this concept is called leveling by DeMacro. Thus, if bubble "A" has two inputs x_1 and x_2 and one output y, then the expanded DFD, that represents "A" should have exactly two external inputs and one external output as shown in figure.

The Level-0 DFD, also called context diagram of the result management system is shown in fig. As the bubbles are decomposed into less and less abstract bubbles, the corresponding data flow may also be needed to be decomposed.

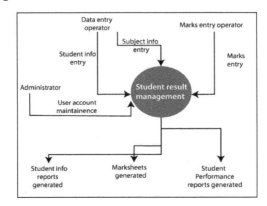

Level-0 DFD of result management system.

1-level DFD

In 1-level DFD, a context diagram is decomposed into multiple bubbles/processes. In this level, we highlight the main objectives of the system and breakdown the high-level process of 0-level DFD into sub processes.

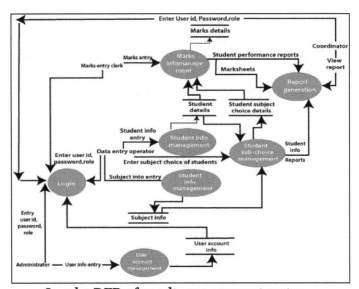

Level-1 DFD of result management system.

2-Level DFD

2-level DFD goes one process deeper into parts of 1-level DFD. It can be used to project or record the specific/necessary detail about the system's functioning.

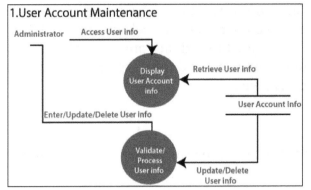

1. User Account Maintenance

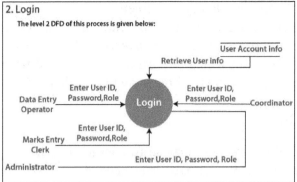

2. Login

The level 2 DFD of this process is given below:

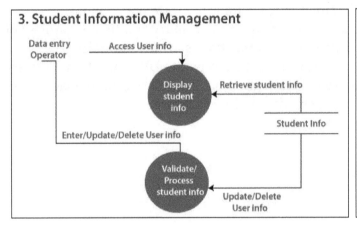

3. Student Information Management

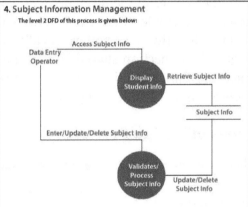

4. Subject Information Management

The level 2 DFD of this process is given below:

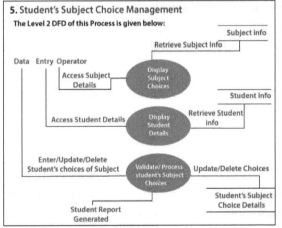

5. Student's Subject Choice Management

The Level 2 DFD of this Process is given below:

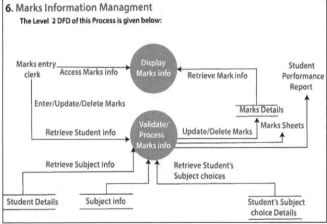

6. Marks Information Managment

The Level 2 DFD of this Process is given below:

Software Design Patterns

A design pattern provides a general reusable solution for the common problems occurs in software design. The patterns typically show relationships and interactions between classes or objects. The idea is to speed up the development process by providing well tested, proven development/design paradigm. Design patterns are programming language independent strategies for solving a common problem. That means a design pattern represents an idea, not a particular implementation. By using the design patterns you can make your code more flexible, reusable and maintainable.

It's not mandatory to implement design patterns in your project always. Design patterns are not meant for project development. Design patterns are meant for common problem-solving. Whenever there is a need, you have to implement a suitable pattern to avoid such problems in the future. To find out which pattern to use. You just have to try to understand the design patterns and its purposes. Only by then you will be able to pick the right one.

Goal

Understand the purpose and usage of each design patterns. So, you will be able to pick and implement the correct pattern as needed.

Example: For example, in many real-world situations, we want to create only one instance of a class. For example, there can be only one active president of the country at a time regardless of personal identity. This pattern is called a Singleton pattern. Other software examples could be a single DB connection shared by multiple objects as creating a separate DB connection for every object may be costly. Similarly, there can be a single configuration manager or error manager in an application that handles all problems instead of creating multiple managers.

Types of Design Patterns

There are mainly three types of design patterns:

Creational

These design patterns are all about class instantiation or object creation. These patterns can be further categorized into Class-creational patterns and object-creational patterns. While class-creation patterns use inheritance effectively in the instantiation process, object-creation patterns use delegation effectively to get the job done.

Creational design patterns are the Factory Method, Abstract Factory, Builder, Singleton, Object Pool, and Prototype.

Use case of creational design pattern:

1. Suppose a developer wants to create a simple DBConnection class to connect to a database and wants to access the database at multiple locations from code, generally what developer will do is create an instance of DBConnection class and use it for doing database operations wherever required. Which results in creating multiple connections from the database as each instance of DBConnection class will have a separate connection to the database. In order to deal with it, we create DBConnection class as a singleton class, so that only one instance of DBConnection is created and a single connection is established. Because we can manage DB Connection via one instance so we can control load balance, unnecessary connections, etc.

2. Suppose you want to create multiple instances of similar kind and want to achieve loose coupling then you can go for Factory pattern. A class implementing factory design pattern works as a bridge between multiple classes. Consider an example of using multiple database servers like SQL Server and Oracle. If you are developing an application using SQL

Server database as back end, but in future need to change database to oracle, you will need to modify all your code, so as factory design patterns maintain loose coupling and easy implementation we should go for factory for achieving loose coupling and creation of similar kind of object.

Structural

These design patterns are about organizing different classes and objects to form larger structures and provide new functionality.

Structural design patterns are Adapter, Bridge, Composite, Decorator, Facade, Flyweight, Private Class Data, and Proxy.

Use Case of Structural Design Pattern

When 2 interfaces are not compatible with each other and want to make establish a relationship between them through an adapter it's called adapter design pattern. Adapter pattern converts the interface of a class into another interface or classes the client expects that is adapter lets classes works together that could not otherwise because of incompatibility. So in these type of incompatible scenarios, we can go for the adapter pattern.

Behavioral

Behavioral patterns are about identifying common communication patterns between objects and realize these patterns.

Behavioral patterns are Chain of responsibility, Command, Interpreter, Iterator, Mediator, Memento, Null Object, Observer, State, Strategy, Template method, Visitor.

Use Case of Behavioral Design Pattern

Template pattern defines the skeleton of an algorithm in an operation deferring some steps to sub-classes, Template method lets subclasses redefine certain steps of an algorithm without changing the algorithm structure. say for an example in your project you want the behavior of the module can be extended, such that we can make the module behave in new and different ways as the requirements of the application change, or to meet the needs of new applications. However, No one is allowed to make source code changes to it. It means you can add but can't modify the structure in those scenarios a developer can approach template design pattern.

Creational Design Patterns

In software engineering, creational design patterns are design patterns that deal with object creation mechanisms, trying to create objects in a manner suitable to the situation. The basic form of object creation could result in design problems or added complexity to the design. Creational design patterns solve this problem by somehow controlling this object creation.

1. Abstract Factory: Creates an instance of several families of classes.

2. Builder: Separates object construction from its representation.

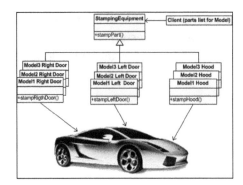

3. Factory Method: Creates an instance of several derived classes.

4. Object Pool: Avoid expensive acquisition and release of resources by recycling objects that are no longer in use.

5. Prototype: A fully initialized instance to be copied or cloned.

6. Singleton: A class of which only a single instance can exist.

Features

1. Sometimes creational patterns are competitors: there are cases when either Prototype or Abstract Factory could be used profitably. At other times they are complementary: Abstract Factory might store a set of Prototypes from which to clone and return product objects, Builder can use one of the other patterns to implement which components get built. Abstract Factory, Builder, and Prototype can use Singleton in their implementation.

2. Abstract Factory, Builder, and Prototype define a factory object that's responsible for knowing and creating the class of product objects, and make it a parameter of the system. Abstract Factory has the factory object producing objects of several classes. Builder has the factory object building a complex product incrementally using a correspondingly complex protocol. Prototype has the factory object (aka prototype) building a product by copying a prototype object.

3. Abstract Factory classes are often implemented with Factory Methods, but they can also be implemented using Prototype.

4. Abstract Factory can be used as an alternative to Facade to hide platform-specific classes.

5. Builder focuses on constructing a complex object step by step. Abstract Factory emphasizes a family of product objects (either simple or complex). Builder returns the product as a final step, but as far as the Abstract Factory is concerned, the product gets returned immediately.

6. Builder is to creation as Strategy is to algorithm.

7. Builder often builds a Composite.

8. Factory Methods are usually called within Template methods.

9. Factory Method: creation through inheritance. Prototype: creation through delegation.

10. Often, designs start out using Factory Method (less complicated, more customizable, sub-classes proliferate) and evolve toward Abstract Factory, Prototype, or Builder (more flexible, more complex) as the designer discovers where more flexibility is needed.

11. Prototype doesn't require subclassing, but it does require an Initialize operation. Factory Method requires subclassing, but doesn't require Initialize.

12. Designs that make heavy use of the Composite and Decorator patterns often can benefit from Prototype as well.

Factory Method

Factory method is a creational design pattern, i.e., related to object creation. In Factory pattern, we create object without exposing the creation logic to client and the client use the same common interface to create new type of object.

The idea is to use a static member-function (static factory method) which creates & returns instances, hiding the details of class modules from user.

A factory pattern is one of the core design principles to create an object, allowing clients to create objects of a library in a way such that it doesn't have tight coupling with the class hierarchy of the library.

What is Meant when we Talk about Library and Clients?

A library is something which is provided by some third party which exposes some public APIs and clients make calls to those public APIs to complete its task. A very simple example can be different kinds of Views provided by Android OS.

Why Factory Pattern?

Let us understand it with an example:

```cpp
// A design without factory pattern
#include <iostream>
using namespace std;


// Library classes
class Vehicle {
public:
    virtual void printVehicle() = 0;
};
class TwoWheeler : public Vehicle {
```

```cpp
public:
    void printVehicle()  {
        cout << "I am two wheeler" << endl;
    }
};
class FourWheeler : public Vehicle {
    public:
    void printVehicle()  {
        cout << "I am four wheeler" << endl;
    }
};


// Client (or user) class
class Client {
public:
    Client(int type)  {

        // Client explicitly creates classes according to type
        if (type == 1)
            pVehicle = new TwoWheeler();
        else if (type == 2)
            pVehicle = new FourWheeler();
        else
            pVehicle = NULL;
    }

    ~Client()   {
        if (pVehicle)
        {
            delete[] pVehicle;
            pVehicle = NULL;
        }
    }
```

```
    Vehicle* getVehicle() {

        return pVehicle;

    }
private:

    Vehicle *pVehicle;

};


// Driver program
int main() {

    Client *pClient = new Client(1);

    Vehicle * pVehicle = pClient->getVehicle();

    pVehicle->printVehicle();

    return 0;

}
```

Output:

```
I am two wheeler
```

What is the Problem with above Design?

As you must have observed in the above example, Client creates objects of either Two Wheeler or Four Wheeler based on some input during constructing its object.

Say, library introduces a new class Three Wheeler to incorporate three wheeler vehicles also. What would happen? Client will end up chaining a new else if in the conditional ladder to create objects of Three Wheeler. Which in turn will need Client to be recompiled. So, each time a new change is made at the library side, Client would need to make some corresponding changes at its end and recompile the code. Sounds bad? This is a very bad practice of design.

How to Avoid the Problem?

The answer is, create a static (or factory) method. Let us see below code.

```
// C++ program to demonstrate factory method design pattern

#include <iostream>

using namespace std;


enum VehicleType {

    VT_TwoWheeler,     VT_ThreeWheeler,     VT_FourWheeler
```

```cpp
};


// Library classes
class Vehicle {
public:
    virtual void printVehicle() = 0;
    static Vehicle* Create(VehicleType type);
};
class TwoWheeler : public Vehicle {
public:
    void printVehicle() {
        cout << "I am two wheeler" << endl;
    }
};
class ThreeWheeler : public Vehicle {
public:
    void printVehicle() {
        cout << «I am three wheeler" << endl;
    }
};
class FourWheeler : public Vehicle {
    public:
    void printVehicle() {
        cout << "I am four wheeler" << endl;
    }
};


// Factory method to create objects of different types.
// Change is required only in this function to create a new object type
Vehicle* Vehicle::Create(VehicleType type) {
    if (type == VT_TwoWheeler)
        return new TwoWheeler();
    else if (type == VT_ThreeWheeler)
```

```
            return new ThreeWheeler();
        else if (type == VT_FourWheeler)
            return new FourWheeler();
        else return NULL;
}


// Client class
class Client {
public:

    // Client doesn't explicitly create objects
    // but passes type to factory method "Create()"
    Client()
    {
        VehicleType type = VT_ThreeWheeler;
        pVehicle = Vehicle::Create(type);
    }
    ~Client() {
        if (pVehicle) {
            delete[] pVehicle;
            pVehicle = NULL;
        }
    }
    Vehicle* getVehicle()  {
        return pVehicle;
    }

private:
    Vehicle *pVehicle;
};

// Driver program
int main() {
```

```
Client *pClient = new Client();

Vehicle * pVehicle = pClient->getVehicle();

pVehicle->printVehicle();

return 0;

}
```

Output:

```
I am three wheeler
```

In the above example, we have totally decoupled the selection of type for object creation from Client. The library is now responsible to decide which object type to create based on an input. Client just needs to make call to library's factory create method and pass the type it wants without worrying about the actual implementation of creation of objects.

Builder

There are several use cases where we have to create a very complex object, which requires different steps and actions for each one. In such cases, the Builder design pattern can be really useful.

The Builder design pattern is a creational design pattern and can be used to create complex objects step by step.

Supposing we have an object with many dependencies and need to acquire each one of these dependencies, certain actions have to be issued. In such cases, we can use the Builder pattern in order to:

- Encapsulate, create, and assemble the parts of a complex object in a separate Builder object.

- Delegate the object creation to a Builder object instead of creating the objects directly.

Imagine the scenario of a backend system that has to compose and send emails.

Creating an email might be a complex procedure. You have to specify the title, set the recipients, add a greeting, and add a closing statement. You might also want to use mustache instead. Needless to say, there is a wide range of options.

Having one class for all the actions needed to create an email might make our class bloated and loose its original purpose.

So, we will start with the class responsible for sending the email.

```
package com.gkatzioura.design.creational.builder;

public class Email {

    private final String title;

    private final String recipients;

    private final String message;

    public Email(String title, String recipients, String message) {
```

```
            this.title = title;

            this.recipients = recipients;

            this.message = message;

    }

    public String getTitle() {

        return title;

    }

    public String getRecipients() {

        return recipients;

    }

    public String getMessage() {

        return message;

    }

    public void send() {

    }

}
```

As you can see, the class contains only three string fields and there is no extra processing on them. So, we shall create a builder class that will handle the message formatting, the recipient representation, and the creation of the Email class.

```
package com.gkatzioura.design.creational.builder;

import java.util.HashSet;

import java.util.Set;

public class EmailBuilder {

    private Set recipients = new HashSet();

    private String title;

    private String greeting;

    private String mainText;

    private String closing;

    public EmailBuilder addRecipient(String recipient) {

        this.recipients.add(recipient);

        return this;

    }

    public EmailBuilder removeRecipient(String recipient) {

        this.recipients.remove(recipient);
```

```
            return this;
        }

    public EmailBuilder setTitle(String title) {
        this.title = title;
        return this;
    }

    public EmailBuilder setGreeting(String greeting) {
        this.greeting = greeting;
        return this;
    }

    public EmailBuilder setMainText(String mainText) {
        this.mainText = mainText;
        return this;
    }

    public EmailBuilder setClosing(String closing) {
        this.closing = closing;
        return this;
    }

    public Email create() {
        String message = greeting+"\n"+mainText+"\n"+closing;
        String recipientSection = commaSeparatedRecipients();
        return new Email(title,recipientSection,message);
    }

    private String commaSeparatedRecipients() {
        StringBuilder sb = new StringBuilder();
        for(String recipient:recipients) {
            sb.append(",").append(recipient);
        }
        return sb.toString().replaceFirst(",","");
    }

}
```

The next step is to make the email creation stricter so that creating an email would only be possible through the Email Builder.

```java
package com.gkatzioura.design.creational.builder;
import java.util.HashSet;
import java.util.Set;
public class Email {
    private final String title;
    private final String recipients;
    private final String message;
    private Email(String title, String recipients, String message) {
        this.title = title;
        this.recipients = recipients;
        this.message = message;
    }
    public String getTitle() {
        return title;
    }
    public String getRecipients() {
        return recipients;
    }
    public String getMessage() {
        return message;
    }
    public void send() {
    }
    public static class EmailBuilder {
        private Set recipients = new HashSet();
        private String title;
        private String greeting;
        private String mainText;
        private String closing;
        public EmailBuilder addRecipient(String recipient) {
            this.recipients.add(recipient);
            return this;
        }
```

```java
    public EmailBuilder removeRecipient(String recipient) {
        this.recipients.remove(recipient);
        return this;
    }

    public EmailBuilder setTitle(String title) {
        this.title = title;
        return this;
    }

    public EmailBuilder setGreeting(String greeting) {
        this.greeting = greeting;
        return this;
    }

    public EmailBuilder setMainText(String mainText) {
        this.mainText = mainText;
        return this;
    }

    public EmailBuilder setClosing(String closing) {
        this.closing = closing;
        return this;
    }

    public Email build() {
        String message = greeting+"\n"+mainText+"\n"+closing;
        String recipientSection = commaSeparatedRecipients();
        return new Email(title,recipientSection,message);
    }

    private String commaSeparatedRecipients() {
        StringBuilder sb = new StringBuilder();
        for(String recipient:recipients) {
            sb.append(",").append(recipient);
        }
        return sb.toString().replaceFirst(",","");
    }

    }

}
```

The end result of using the Builder pattern for creating an email will look like this:

```
Email email = new Email.EmailBuilder()

    .addRecipient("john@Doe.com")

    .setMainText("Check the builder pattern")

    .setGreeting("Hi John!")

    .setClosing("Regards")

    .setTitle("Builder pattern resources")

    .build();
```

To summarize, by using the Builder design pattern, we were able to create a complex object and its complex parts.

Abstract Factory

Abstract Factory patterns work around a super-factory which creates other factories. This factory is also called as factory of factories. This type of design pattern comes under creational pattern as this pattern provides one of the best ways to create an object.

In Abstract Factory pattern an interface is responsible for creating a factory of related objects without explicitly specifying their classes. Each generated factory can give the objects as per the Factory pattern.

Implementation

We are going to create a Shape and Color interfaces and concrete classes implementing these interfaces. We create an abstract factory class Abstract Factory as next step. Factory classes Shape Factory and Color Factory are defined where each factory extends Abstract Factory. A factory creator/generator class Factory Producer is created.

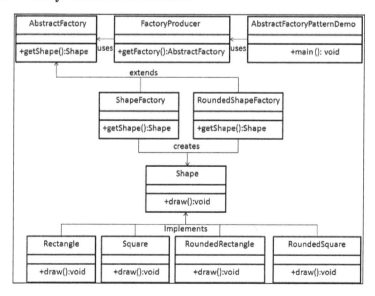

For our example of an AbStract Factory Pattern, we will use Factory Producer to get a Abstract Factory object. It will pass information (CIRCLE / RECTANGLE / SQUARE for Shape) to Abstract Factory to get the type of object it needs. It also passes information (RED / GREEN / BLUE for Color) to Abstract Factory to get the type of object it needs.

Step 1

Create an interface for Shapes and Colors.

Shape.java

```
public interface Shape {

    void draw();

}
```

Step 2

Create concrete classes implementing the same interface.

RoundedRectangle.java

```
public class RoundedRectangle implements Shape {

    @Override

    public void draw() {

        System.out.println("Inside RoundedRectangle::draw() method.");

    }

}
```

RoundedSquare.java

```
public class RoundedSquare implements Shape {

    @Override

    public void draw() {

        System.out.println("Inside RoundedSquare::draw() method.");

    }

}
```

Rectangle.java

```
public class Rectangle implements Shape {

    @Override

    public void draw() {

        System.out.println("Inside Rectangle::draw() method.");

    }

}
```

Step 3

Create an Abstract class to get factories for Normal and Rounded Shape Objects.

AbstractFactory.java

```java
public abstract class AbstractFactory {

    abstract Shape getShape(String shapeType) ;

}
```

Step 4

Create Factory classes extending AbstractFactory to generate object of concrete class based on given information.

ShapeFactory.java

```java
public class ShapeFactory extends AbstractFactory {

    @Override
    public Shape getShape(String shapeType){
        if(shapeType.equalsIgnoreCase("RECTANGLE")){

            return new Rectangle();

        }else if(shapeType.equalsIgnoreCase("SQUARE")){

            return new Square();

        }
        return null;

    }

}
```

RoundedShapeFactory.java

```java
public class RoundedShapeFactory extends AbstractFactory {

    @Override
    public Shape getShape(String shapeType){
        if(shapeType.equalsIgnoreCase("RECTANGLE")){

            return new RoundedRectangle();

        }else if(shapeType.equalsIgnoreCase("SQUARE")){

            return new RoundedSquare();

        }
        return null;

    }

}
```

Step 5

Create a Factory generator/producer class to get factories by passing information such as Shape

FactoryProducer.java

```
public class FactoryProducer {
    public static AbstractFactory getFactory(boolean rounded){
        if(rounded){
            return new RoundedShapeFactory();
        }else{
            return new ShapeFactory();
        }
    }
}
```

Step 6

Use the FactoryProducer to get AbstractFactory in order to get factories of concrete classes by passing information such as type.

AbstractFactoryPatternDemo.java

```
public class AbstractFactoryPatternDemo {
    public static void main(String[] args) {
        //get rounded shape factory
        AbstractFactory shapeFactory = FactoryProducer.getFactory(false);
        //get an object of Shape Rounded Rectangle
        Shape shape1 = shapeFactory.getShape("RECTANGLE");
        //call draw method of Shape Rectangle
        shape1.draw();
        //get an object of Shape Rounded Square
        Shape shape2 = shapeFactory.getShape("SQUARE");
        //call draw method of Shape Square
        shape2.draw();
        //get rounded shape factory
        AbstractFactory shapeFactory1 = FactoryProducer.getFactory(true);
        //get an object of Shape Rectangle
        Shape shape3 = shapeFactory1.getShape("RECTANGLE");
```

```
//call draw method of Shape Rectangle

shape3.draw();

//get an object of Shape Square

Shape shape4 = shapeFactory1.getShape("SQUARE");

//call draw method of Shape Square

shape4.draw();


    }

}
```

Step 7

Verify the output.

```
Inside Rectangle::draw() method.

Inside Square::draw() method.

Inside RoundedRectangle::draw() method.

Inside RoundedSquare::draw() method.
```

Structural Design Patterns

Structural Design Patterns are Design Patterns that ease the design by identifying a simple way to realize relationships between entities.

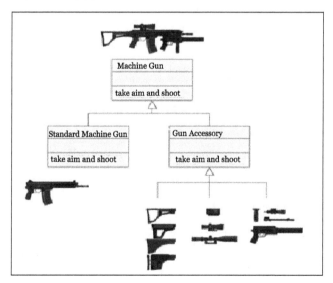

- Adapter: Match interfaces of different classes.

- Bridge: Separates an object's interface from its implementation.

- Composite: A tree structure of simple and composite objects.

- Decorator: Add responsibilities to objects dynamically.

- Facade: A single class that represents an entire subsystem.

- Flyweight: A fine-grained instance used for efficient sharing.

- Private Class Data: Restricts accessor/mutator access.

- Proxy: An object representing another object.

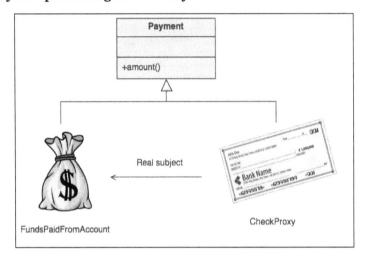

Features

1. Adapter makes things work after they are designed; Bridge makes them work before they are.

2. Bridge is designed up-front to let the abstraction and the implementation vary independently. Adapter is retrofitted to make unrelated classes work together.

3. Adapter provides a different interface to its subject. Proxy provides the same interface. Decorator provides an enhanced interface.

4. Adapter changes an object's interface; Decorator enhances an object's responsibilities.

5. Decorator is thus more transparent to the client. As a consequence, Decorator supports recursive composition, which isn't possible with pure Adapters.

6. Composite and Decorator have similar structure diagrams, reflecting the fact that both rely on recursive composition to organize an open-ended number of objects.

7. Composite can be traversed with Iterator. Visitor can apply an operation over a Composite. Composite could use Chain of responsibility to let components access global properties through their parent. It could also use Decorator to override these properties on parts of the composition. It could use Observer to tie one object structure to another and State to let a component change its behavior as its state changes.

8. Composite can let you compose a Mediator out of smaller pieces through recursive composition.

9. Decorator lets you change the skin of an object. Strategy lets you change the guts.

10. Decorator is designed to let you add responsibilities to objects without subclassing. Composite's focus is not on embellishment but on representation. These intents are distinct but complementary. Consequently, Composite and Decorator are often used in concert.

11. Decorator and Proxy have different purposes but similar structures. Both describe how to provide a level of indirection to another object, and the implementations keep a reference to the object to which they forward requests.

12. Facade defines a new interface, whereas Adapter reuses an old interface. Remember that Adapter makes two existing interfaces work together as opposed to defining an entirely new one.

13. Facade objects are often Singleton because only one Facade object is required.

14. Mediator is similar to Facade in that it abstracts functionality of existing classes. Mediator abstracts/centralizes arbitrary communication between colleague objects, it routinely "adds value", and it is known/referenced by the colleague objects. In contrast, Facade defines a simpler interface to a subsystem, it doesn't add new functionality, and it is not known by the subsystem classes.

15. Abstract Factory can be used as an alternative to Facade to hide platform-specific classes.

16. Whereas Flyweight shows how to make lots of little objects, Facade shows how to make a single object represent an entire subsystem.

17. Flyweight is often combined with Composite to implement shared leaf nodes.

18. Flyweight explains when and how State objects can be shared.

Adapter

This pattern is easy to understand as the real world is full of adapters. For example consider a USB to Ethernet adapter. We need this when we have an Ethernet interface on one end and USB on the other. Since they are incompatible with each other. We use an adapter that converts one to other. This example is pretty analogous to Object Oriented Adapters. In design, adapters are used when we have a class (Client) expecting some type of object and we have an object (Adaptee) offering the same features but exposing a different interface.

To use an adapter:

1. The client makes a request to the adapter by calling a method on it using the target interface.

2. The adapter translates that request on the adaptee using the adaptee interface.

3. Client receives the results of the call and is unaware of adapter's presence.

The adapter pattern converts the interface of a class into another interface clients expect. Adapter lets classes work together that couldn't otherwise because of incompatible interfaces.

Class, Diagram

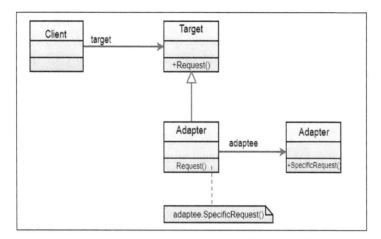

The client sees only the target interface and not the adapter. The adapter implements the target interface. Adapter delegates all requests to Adaptee.

Example: Suppose you have a Bird class with fly( ), and makeSound( )methods. And also a Toy-Duck class with squeak( ) method. Let's assume that you are short on ToyDuck objects and you would like to use Bird objects in their place. Birds have some similar functionality but implement a different interface, so we can't use them directly. So we will use adapter pattern. Here our client would be Toy Duck and adaptee would be Bird.

Below is Java implementation of it.

```
// Java implementation of Adapter pattern


interface Bird

{

    // birds implement Bird interface that allows

    // them to fly and make sounds adaptee interface

    public void fly();

    public void makeSound();

}


class Sparrow implements Bird

{

    // a concrete implementation of bird

    public void fly()

    {
```

```
        System.out.println("Flying");

    }
    public void makeSound()
    {
        System.out.println("Chirp Chirp");
    }
}


interface ToyDuck
{
    // target interface
    // toyducks dont fly they just make
    // squeaking sound
    public void squeak();
}


class PlasticToyDuck implements ToyDuck
{
    public void squeak()
    {
        System.out.println("Squeak");
    }
}


class BirdAdapter implements ToyDuck
{
    // You need to implement the interface your
    // client expects to use.
    Bird bird;
    public BirdAdapter(Bird bird)
    {
        // we need reference to the object we
        // are adapting
```

```java
        this.bird = bird;
    }


    public void squeak()
    {
        // translate the methods appropriately
        bird.makeSound();
    }
}


class Main
{
    public static void main(String args[])
    {
        Sparrow sparrow = new Sparrow();
        ToyDuck toyDuck = new PlasticToyDuck();

        // Wrap a bird in a birdAdapter so that it
        // behaves like toy duck
        ToyDuck birdAdapter = new BirdAdapter(sparrow);

        System.out.println("Sparrow...");
        sparrow.fly();
        sparrow.makeSound();

        System.out.println("ToyDuck...");
        toyDuck.squeak();

        // toy duck behaving like a bird
        System.out.println("BirdAdapter...");
        birdAdapter.squeak();
    }
}
```

Output:

```
Sparrow...

Flying

Chirp Chirp

ToyDuck...

Squeak

BirdAdapter...

Chirp Chirp
```

Explanation: Suppose we have a bird that can make Sound( ), and we have a plastic toy duck that can squeak( ). Now suppose our client changes the requirement and he wants the toy Duck to make Sound than?

Simple solution is that we will just change the implementation class to the new adapter class and tell the client to pass the instance of the bird (which wants to squeak( )) to that class.

- Before : Toy Duck toy Duck = new Plastic Toy Duck( );

- After : Toy Duck toy Duck = new Bird Adapter(sparrow);

You can see that by changing just one line the toy Duck can now do Chirp Chirp.

Object Adapter vs. Class Adapter

The adapter pattern we have implemented above is called Object Adapter Pattern because the adapter holds an instance of adaptee. There is also another type called Class Adapter Pattern which use inheritance instead of composition but you require multiple inheritance to implement it.

Class diagram of Class Adapter Pattern

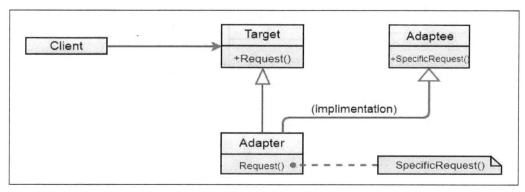

Here instead of having an adaptee object inside adapter (composition) to make use of its functionality adapter inherits the adaptee.

Since multiple inheritances is not supported by many languages including java and is associated with many problems we have not shown implementation using class adapter pattern.

Advantages

- Helps achieve reusability and flexibility.

- Client class is not complicated by having to use a different interface and can use polymorphism to swap between different implementations of adapters.

Disadvantages

- All requests are forwarded, so there is a slight increase in the overhead.

- Sometimes many adaptations are required along an adapter chain to reach the type which is required.

Proxy

In proxy pattern, a class represents functionality of another class. This type of design pattern comes under structural pattern.

In proxy pattern, we create object having original object to interface its functionality to outer world.

Implementation

We are going to create an Image interface and concrete classes implementing the Image interface. Proxy Image is a proxy class to reduce memory footprint of Real Image object loading.

For our example of a ProxyPattern class, will use *Proxy Image* to get an *Image* object to load and display as it needs.

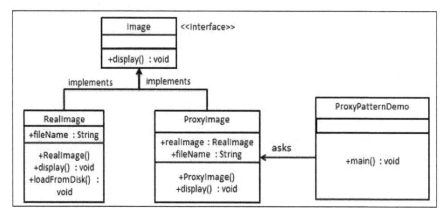

Step 1

Create an interface.

Image.java

```
public interface Image {
    void display();
}
```

Step 2

Create concrete classes implementing the same interface.

RealImage.java

```java
public class RealImage implements Image {

    private String fileName;

    public RealImage(String fileName){
        this.fileName = fileName;
        loadFromDisk(fileName);
    }

    @Override
    public void display() {
        System.out.println("Displaying " + fileName);
    }

    private void loadFromDisk(String fileName){
        System.out.println("Loading " + fileName);
    }
}
```

ProxyImage.java

```java
public class ProxyImage implements Image{

    private RealImage realImage;
    private String fileName;

    public ProxyImage(String fileName){
        this.fileName = fileName;
    }

    @Override
    public void display() {
```

```
        if(realImage == null){

            realImage = new RealImage(fileName);

        }

        realImage.display();

    }

}
```

Step 3

Use the ProxyImage to get object of RealImage class when required.

ProxyPatternDemo.java

```
public class ProxyPatternDemo {

    public static void main(String[] args) {
        Image image = new ProxyImage("test_10mb.jpg");


        //image will be loaded from disk
        image.display();
        System.out.println("");


        //image will not be loaded from disk
        image.display();
    }

}
```

Step 4

Verify the output.

```
Loading test_10mb.jpg
Displaying test_10mb.jpg
Displaying test_10mb.jpg
```

Behavioral Design Patterns

Behavioural design patterns are design patterns that identify common communication patterns between objects and realize these patterns. By doing so, these patterns increase flexibility in carrying out this communication.

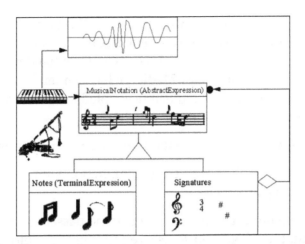

- Chain of responsibility: A way of passing a request between a chain of objects.

- Command: Encapsulate a command request as an object.

- Interpreter: A way to include language elements in a program.

- Iterator: Sequentially access the elements of a collection.

- Mediator: Defines simplified communication between classes.

- Memento: Capture and restore an object's internal state.

- Null Object: Designed to act as a default value of an object.

- Observer: A way of notifying change to a number of classes.

- State: Alter an object's behavior when its state changes.

- Strategy: Encapsulates an algorithm inside a class.

- Template method: Defer the exact steps of an algorithm to a subclass.

- Visitor: Defines a new operation to a class without change.

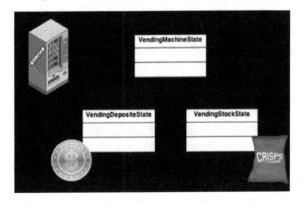

Features

1. Behavioral patterns are concerned with the assignment of responsibilities between objects, or, encapsulating behavior in an object and delegating requests to it.

2. Chain of responsibility, Command, Mediator, and Observer, address how you can decouple senders and receivers, but with different trade-offs. Chain of responsibility passes a sender request along a chain of potential receivers. Command normally specifies a sender-receiver connection with a subclass. Mediator has senders and receivers reference each other indirectly. Observer defines a much decoupled interface that allows for multiple receivers to be configured at run-time.

3. Chain of responsibility can use Command to represent requests as objects.

4. Chain of responsibility is often applied in conjunction with Composite. There, a component's parent can act as its successor.

5. Command and Memento act as magic tokens to be passed around and invoked at a later time. In Command, the token represents a request; in Memento, it represents the internal state of an object at a particular time. Polymorphism is important to Command, but not to Memento because its interface is so narrow that a memento can only be passed as a value.

6. Command can use Memento to maintain the state required for an undo operation.

7. MacroCommands can be implemented with Composite.

8. A Command that must be copied before being placed on a history list acts as a Prototype.

9. Interpreter can use State to define parsing contexts.

10. The abstract syntax tree of Interpreter is a Composite (therefore Iterator and Visitor are also applicable).

11. Terminal symbols within Interpreter's abstract syntax tree can be shared with Flyweight.

12. Iterator can traverse a Composite. Visitor can apply an operation over a Composite.

13. Polymorphic Iterators rely on Factory Methods to instantiate the appropriate Iterator subclass.

14. Mediator and Observer are competing patterns. The difference between them is that Observer distributes communication by introducing "observer" and "subject" objects, whereas a Mediator object encapsulates the communication between other objects. We've found it easier to make reusable Observers and Subjects than to make reusable Mediators.

15. On the other hand, Mediator can leverage Observer for dynamically registering colleagues and communicating with them.

16. Mediator is similar to Facade in that it abstracts functionality of existing classes. Mediator abstracts/centralizes arbitrary communication between colleague objects, it routinely "adds value", and it is known/referenced by the colleague objects (i.e. it defines a multidirectional protocol). In contrast, Facade defines a simpler interface to a subsystem, it doesn't add new functionality, and it is not known by the subsystem classes (i.e. it defines a unidirectional protocol where it makes requests of the subsystem classes but not vice versa).

17. Memento is often used in conjunction with Iterator. An Iterator can use a Memento to capture the state of iteration. The Iterator stores the Memento internally.

18. State is like Strategy except in its intent.

19. Flyweight explains when and how State objects can be shared.

20. State objects are often Singletons.

21. Strategy lets you change the guts of an object. Decorator lets you change the skin.

22. Strategy is to algorithm. as Builder is to creation.

23. Strategy has 2 different implementations; the first is similar to State. The difference is in binding times (Strategy is a bind-once pattern, whereas State is more dynamic).

24. Strategy objects often make good Flyweights.

25. Strategy is like Template method except in its granularity.

26. Template method uses inheritance to vary part of an algorithm. Strategy uses delegation to vary the entire algorithm.

27. The Visitor pattern is like a more powerful Command pattern because the visitor may initiate whatever is appropriate for the kind of object it encounters.

Command

The command pattern is quite different from the CoR pattern since it helps us delegate an action/request to another object that is capable of executing it. Thus, there is no direct execution whatsoever.

For the command pattern, we need an object to encapsulate all the information needed to perform an action or trigger an event sometime later.

One of the scenarios where it might seem very familiar is when it comes to queues and consuming those messages. This is pretty much carried out the same way that the elastic beanstalk workers consume messages from queues.

Each message in a queue contains a command, and the code that handles that message has to execute it.

Let's do this with an example from the betting industry. We are going to have some a bet backed and sent over to our booking system.

```
So, let's create the bet class.
package com.gkatzioura.design.behavioural.command;
public class Bet {
    private final String match;
    private final Integer amount;
    public Bet(final String match, final Integer amount) {
        this.match = match;
```

```java
        this.amount = amount;
    }

    public String getMatch() {

        return match;

    }

    public Integer getAmount() {

        return amount;

    }

}
```

Now, let's add a class that contains our bet actions. This is going to be our BetBook.

```java
package com.gkatzioura.design.behavioural.command;

public class BetBook {

    public void addBacking(String match, Integer amount) {

        /**

         * Add the backing to the book

         */

    }

}
```

It is time for us to specify the bet command. The bet command is going to be applied to our BetBook.

```java
package com.gkatzioura.design.behavioural.command;

public interface BetCommand {

    void applyTo(BetBook betBook);

}
```

This brings us to the Backing command.

```java
package com.gkatzioura.design.behavioural.command;

public class BackingCommand implements BetCommand {

    private final Bet bet;

    public BackingCommand(final Bet bet) {

        this.bet = bet;

    }
```

```
    @Override

    public void applyTo(BetBook betBook) {

        betBook.addBacking(bet.getMatch(),bet.getAmount());

    }

}
```

So, let's put them all together.

```
package com.gkatzioura.design.behavioural.command;

import java.util.ArrayList;

import java.util.List;

public class Command {

    public static void main(String[] args) {

        List<BetCommand> betCommands = new ArrayList<>();

        betCommands.add(new BackingCommand(new Bet("match1",10)));

        betCommands.add(new BackingCommand(new Bet("match2",11)));

        BetBook betBook = new BetBook();

        betCommands.forEach(bc->bc.applyTo(betBook));

    }

}
```

We just gathered our bet commands.

Iterator

Iterator Design Pattern is one of the Behavioural design patterns in Java. It is used for traversing through the collection of data in a particular class.

This pattern hides the actual implementation of traversal through the collection. The application programs just use iterator methods for different purposes. Iterator pattern allows accessing the elements of a collection object in a sequential manner without knowledge of its structure. Key points to remember about this interface are:

- This pattern is used when you foresee a collection is traversed with different types of criteria.
- The collection object should be accessed and traversed without exposing its data structure.
- New traversal operations should be defined for collection object without changing its interface.

Iterator Design Pattern by Example

To understand we will consider a simple example of Book Service. We will also implement a custom iterator which will traverse based on the publisher of the book.

First things first, let us define our iterator interface.

BookIterator.java

```java
public interface BookIterator {


    public boolean hasMore();


    public Book next();
}
```

Our custom iterator interface has 2 methods. One will determine if there are any more elements to traverse. The other method next() will give us actual element.

As we are iterating over books, we will define simple POJO as:

Book.java

```java
public class Book {


    private String name;
    private String publication;


    //Constructor; Getters; Setters;
}
```

Our base classes are ready, let's define BookService and its custom iterator:

BookService.java

```java
public class BookService {


    private List<Book> books;


    public BookIterator getIterator(String publication) {
        return new BookIteratorImpl(books, publication);
    }


    private class BookIteratorImpl implements BookIterator {
```

```
        private String publicationCheck;
        private List<Book> listOfBooks;
        private int index;


        public BookIteratorImpl(List<Book> books, String pubCheck) {
                this.listOfBooks = books;
                this.publicationCheck = pubCheck;
        }


        @Override
        public boolean hasMore() {
                while(index < listOfBooks.size()) {
                        Book buk = this.listOfBooks.get(index);
                        if(buk.getPublication().equalsIgnoreCase(publica-
tionCheck)) {

                                return true;
                        } else {
                                index++;
                        }
                }
                return false;
        }


        @Override
        public Book next() {
                Book buk = this.listOfBooks.get(index);
                index++;
                return buk;
        }
    }


    public BookService() {
        books = new ArrayList<Book>();
    }
```

```
public List<Book> getBooks() {

        return books;

}


public void setBooks(List<Book> books) {

        this.books = books;

}

}
```

Please note that this custom iterator is specific to this type of collection. Hence we have added that as a private class to our main class.

The custom iterator accepts publisher name to check and iterate over only books of that publisher.

Running the Example

```
IteratorPatternDemo
public class IteratorPatternDemo {
        public static void main(String[] args) {
                List<Book> books = new ArrayList<Book>();
                books.add(new Book("Java", "Pub A"));
                books.add(new Book("C++", "Pub B"));
                books.add(new Book("PHP", "Pub A"));
                books.add(new Book("Kotlin", "Pub B"));
                books.add(new Book("Kafka", "Pub A"));
                books.add(new Book("Salesforce", "Pub C"));

                BookService bs = new BookService();
                bs.getBooks().addAll(books);


                System.out.println("List of Books from Publisher B");


                BookIterator bi = bs.getIterator("Pub C");
                while (bi.hasMore()) {
                        Book b = bi.next();
                        System.out.println("--> " + b);
```

```
        }

        System.out.println("\nList of Books from Publisher B");


        bi = bs.getIterator("Pub B");
        while (bi.hasMore()) {
            Book b = bi.next();
            System.out.println("--> " + b);
        }


    }
}
```

During our test run, we have prepared a list of few books and trying to iterate over them. The output:

```
List of Books from Publisher C
--> Book[Salesforce,Pub C]

List of Books from Publisher B
--> Book[C++,Pub B]
--> Book[Kotlin,Pub B]
```

Advantages

- Iterator design pattern hides the actual implementation of traversal through the collection and client programs just use iterator methods.
- The iterator pattern can be implemented in a customized way in Java according to need.
- We can use several iterators on the same collection.

Programming Language Considerations

When planning a software solution, you have many different programming languages to choose from, and it's easy to get lost in the intricacies of each one. Your choice of language can depend on many factors. If it's for a personal project or hobby, you may settle for a language you know. If your choice depends on available resources, you might end up with really cryptic approaches. Or, you could spend a lot of time developing reusable components, which can cause the documentation to become a nightmare.

Factors to Consider

There isn't just one factor to think about when choosing a programming language. For example, while developing a dynamic web page, you might consider JavaServer Pages (JSP)/servlets as the best option, and others might prefer using PHP or a similar scripting language. No single language is the "best choice." Though you might give preference to certain factors, such as performance and security in enterprise applications, other factors, such as fewer lines of code, might be lower priorities. There's always some trade-off.

After you're given a project or assignment, there's often preparation work to be done before solving the actual problem. The choice of language is by far the most overlooked component of this preparation.

When selecting a language for a personal project, you may pick a personal favorite. Lines of code are important here; the obvious choice is a language that can get the work done in 10 instead of 20 lines of code. You want to get the solution out first, and then worry about the neatness, or performance.

For projects built for a large organization, it's a different scenario. Teams will build components that are going to interact and interconnect with each other to solve a particular problem. The choice of language might involve factors such as how easily the program can be ported to a different platform or the availability of resources.

Selecting the right programming language can yield solutions that are concise, easy to debug, easy to extend, easy to document, and easy to fix. Factors to consider when selecting a programming language are:

- The targeted platform
- The elasticity of a language
- The time to production
- The performance
- The support and community

Targeted Platform

The most important factor to consider is the platform where the program will run. Think in terms of the Java language and C. If the program is written in C and needs to be run on Windows and Linux machines, it would require platform compilers and two different executables. With the Java language, the byte code generated would be enough to run the program on any machine with a Java Virtual Machine (JVM) installed.

A very similar argument applies for websites. They should all look and work the same across all browsers. Using CSS3 tags, HTML5, without checking browser compatibility, will cause the same site to look and behave differently across browsers.

Elasticity

The "elasticity" of a language is the ease with which new features can be added to the existing program. Elasticity can involve adding a new set of functions, or using an existing library to add a new feature. Consider the following questions related to elasticity.

- Can I start using a capability of the language without including a new library?

- If not, is the capability available in the language library?

- If it's not a native capability and not available as a library, what is the effort to build the features from scratch?

Before making a decision, you should know how the program has been designed and what features have been set aside as future improvements.

Though a comparison of these languages is not technically correct, consider Perl and Python. Perl has regular expression support built in as a ready-to-use feature. In the case of Python, you have to import the re module from the standard library.

Time to Production

The time to production is the time it takes to make the program go live—when the code is production-ready and will work the way it's intended. The presentation logic should be added to the control logic when calculating time to production.

Time to production is very dependent on the size of the code. Theoretically, the easier it is to learn a language, the smaller the amount of code and, hence, less time to go live.

For example, a content management site can be developed using PHP scripts in days compared to servlets code that can take months, assuming you are learning both languages from scratch.

Performance

You can squeeze only so much performance out of a program and a platform, and the language used to develop the program affects performance. There are many studies comparing how fast programming languages are in the same environment. You can see different computer benchmarks to use as a reference, though the figures are not for concrete assessments of the performance of any language.

Consider a web application written in both Java code and Python. The performance data, as shown in the benchmark, would lead you to conclude that, given similar environments, the application written in the Java language should run faster than the one written in Python. But what about the environment itself? If the environment is an x86 Ubuntu Intel Q6600 one core, it's a fair game because the computational power is limited. What if the web application is in the cloud, running on Google App Engine? You now have access to virtually unlimited processing power, and both the programs are going to return results at almost the same time. The choice factor now revolves around lines of code and maintainability.

The performance of a language should matter when the target environment doesn't offer much scope for scaling. Hand-held devices are an example of such an environment.

Support and Community

Just as good software needs a community following to help it grow, a programming language should also have a strong community behind it. A language with an active forum is likely to be more popular than even a great language that doesn't have help at hand.

Community support generates wikis, forums, tutorials, and, most importantly, additional libraries that help the language to grow. Gone are the days when people operate in silos. People don't want to skim through all the documentation to get one minor problem solved. If a language has a good following, the chances are good that someone else faced your same issue and wrote about it in a wiki or forum.

Perl is a good example of the importance of community. The Comprehensive Perl Archive Network (CPAN) is a community-driven effort. CPAN's main purpose is to help programmers locate modules and programs not included in the Perl standard distribution. Its structure is decentralized; authors maintain and improve their own modules. Forking, and creating competing modules for the same task or purpose, are common.

Scenarios

The project scenarios in this section illustrate different factors that affect the decision-making process when choosing a language.

REST service for add operation

- A simple feed reader

- Enterprise applications

- Research projects

- REST service for add operation

This scenario is for a service that will do addition in the format of a REST service. You'll invoke a URL, http://<url>?num1=number1&num2=number2, and the result should contain the sum of the two numbers passed to it. You could write the program using different languages. The example here uses JSP, as shown in Listing 1, and PHP, as shown in Listing 2. The JSP program was written in the Eclipse IDE.

Listing 1: REST service using JSP

```
1    <%@ page language="java" contentType="text/html; charset=ISO-8859-1"
2    pageEncoding="ISO-8859-1"%>
3    <!DOCTYPE html PUBLIC "-//W3C//DTD HTML 4.01 Transitional//EN"
4    "http://www.w3.org/TR/html4/loose.dtd">
5    <html>
6    <head>
7    <meta http-equiv="Content-Type" content="text/html; charset=ISO-8859-1">
8    <title>Sum</title>
```

```
9    </head>

10   <body>

11       <% if (request.getParameter("num1") == null ||

12       request.getParameter("num2") == null) { %>

13          <p>

14               <b>Wrong URL!!!</b>

15          </p>

16          <p>

17               <b>Enter URL in this format: </b>

18               <i>

19               http://&lt;url&gt;?num1=number1&amp;num2=number2</i>

20          </p>

21      <% } else { %>

22          <b>Number 1:</b>

23          <i><%= request.getParameter("num1") %></i>

24          <br>

25          <b>Number 2:</b>

26          <i><%= request.getParameter("num2") %></i>

27          <br>

28          <b>Sum:</b>

29          <i><%= Integer.parseInt(request.getParameter("num1")) +

30          Integer.parseInt(request.getParameter("num2")) %></i>

31          <br>

32      <% } %>

33   </body>

34   </html>
```

Listing 2 shows the same program in PHP.

Listing 2: REST service using PHP

```
1    <!DOCTYPE html PUBLIC "-//W3C//DTD HTML 4.01 Transitional//EN"

2    "http://www.w3.org/TR/html4/loose.dtd">

3    <html>
```

```
4    <head>

5    <meta http-equiv="Content-Type" content="text/html; charset=ISO-8859-1">

6    <title>Sum</title>

7    </head>

8    <body>

9        <?php if ($_GET["num1"] == NULL || $_GET["num2"] == NULL) { ?>

10       <p><b>Wrong URL!!!</b></p>

11       <p>

12           <b>Enter URL in this format: </b>

13           <i>http://&lt;url&gt;?num1=number1&amp;num2=number2</i>

14       </p>

15       <?php } else { ?>

16           <b>Number 1:</b>

17           <i><?= $_GET["num1"] ?></i>

18           <br>

19           <b>Number 2:</b>

20           <i><?= $_GET["num2"] ?></i>

21           <br>

22           <b>Sum:</b>

23           <i><?= $_GET["num1"] + $_GET["num2"] ?></i>

24           <br>

25       <?php } ?>

26   </body>

27   </html>
```

There isn't much difference between the two examples. The program itself doesn't explore all the capabilities of the two languages. It demonstrates that, when it comes to basics, both the languages are at par.

Features of JSP allow it to be used more at an enterprise level. For example, with JSP, the very first time the program is called it's loaded into the memory as a servlet. For every subsequent request the program in the memory is called, giving better response time with subsequent calls. It's also ideal in a Java environment. With PHP, however, each time the program is called it's loaded into the memory, which might increase response time for critical applications.

Another notable feature that makes JSP a better choice in an enterprise is its multi-threading capabilities. PHP has no built-in support for multi-threading.

A simple Feed Reader

The goal in this scenario is to provide the program with a feed link. The program has to get the feed and list all the titles in the feed. To make it a bit more interesting, you'll subscribe to a JSON-formatted feed and not RSS.

The code snipped in Listing 3 is from O'Reilly and is written in Java code.

Listing 3: Feed reader using Java code

```
1    import java.io.InputStream;
2    import java.net.URL;
3    import java.net.URLConnection;
4    import org.apache.commons.io.IOUtils;
5    import net.sf.json.JSONArray;
6    import net.sf.json.JSONObject;
7    import net.sf.json.JSONSerializer;
8
9    public class JsonParser {
10       public static void main(String[] args) throws Exception {
11           String urlString =
12   "http://pipes.yahoo.com/pipes/pipe.run?_id=df36e60df711191549cf529e1df96884&
13   _render=json&
14   textinput1=and&urlinput1=http%3A%2F%2Ffeeds.wired.com%2Fwired%2Findex";
15           URL url = new URL(urlString);
16           URLConnection urlCon = url.openConnection();
17           InputStream is = urlCon.getInputStream();
18           String jsonTxt = IOUtils.toString(is);
19           JSONObject json = (JSONObject) JSONSerializer.toJSON(jsonTxt);
20           JSONObject value = json.getJSONObject("value");
21           JSONArray items = value.getJSONArray("items");
22           String title;
23           for (Object item : items) {
24               title=((JSONObject)item).getString("title");
25               System.out.println("\n" + title);
26           }
27       }
28   }
```

Listing 4 shows the program in Python.

Listing 4: Feed reader using Python

```
1   #!/usr/bin/python

2   import urllib.request

3   url = "http://pipes.yahoo.com/pipes/pipe.run?

4      _id=df36e60df711191549cf529e1df96884&_render=json&

5      textinput1=and&urlinput1=http%3A%2F%2Ffeeds.wired.com%2Fwired%2Findex"

6   HTTPdata = urllib.request.urlopen(url)

7   json_data = eval(HTTPdata.read())

8   for item in json_data['value']['items']:

9       print (item['title'])
```

The Python program can be further abridged into just three lines. Retain the first two lines of Listing 4, and replace the rest of the code with the line in Listing 5.

Listing 5: Abridged 3rd line

```
1   for item in eval((urllib.request.urlopen("http://pipes.yahoo.com/pipes/pipe.run?

2      _id=df36e60df711191549cf529e1df96884&_render=json&textinput1=and&

3      urlinput1=http%3A%2F%2Ffeeds.wired.com%2Fwired%2Findex"))

4      .read()))['value']['items']:print (item['title'])
```

The example application showed the elasticity of these languages. None of them had native support for all the required libraries; you have to import the necessary packages. With Python, it was even simpler because you could manipulate JSON by default. With Java code, it was more difficult because you had to get the JSON libraries and their dependencies to make the program work.

Enterprise Applications

With enterprise applications, designers and programmers need to walk a tightrope when it comes to performance, security, maintainability, and development time. It's not just about using the programming language that can get you the best performance figures. Other important factors include: time to production, elasticity, and how well the program can integrate with the existing infrastructure.

The environment in which the program will be used also plays an important part. Programs written at an enterprise level are never stand-alone. Each program becomes part of an even larger goal, so interoperability becomes a factor.

Imagine that an enterprise with its web services implemented in Java code wants to add WebSphere MQ as a reliable platform. It doesn't make any sense to use the C APIs of WebSphere MQ to write the application; the choice would have to be Java code.

Types of Programming Languages

Language is the medium of communication to share ideas, opinion with each other. For an example, if we want to communicate with someone, we need a language it may be English, Hindi, Spanish or another language. But you need at least one language to communicate with someone (human/person).

Programming Language

To communicate with a person, you need a language. Same if you need to communicate with the computer, you need a programming language. Without any programming language you cannot communicate with the computer.

Thus, programming language is the medium of communication between you (a person) and a computer system. It is the set of some instructions written in a specific style (coding) to instruct the computer to do some specific task.

There are basically three types of computer programming languages, they are:

1. Low level programming languages.

2. High level programming languages.

3. Middle level programming languages.

Low Level Programming Languages

These are machine dependent programming languages such as Binary (Machine code) and Assembly language.

Since computer only understand the Binary language that means instructions in the form of 0's and 1's (Signals - that can be either High or Low), so these programming languages are the best way to give signals (Binary Instructions) to the computer directly.

Machine Code (Binary Language) does not need any interpreter or compiler to convert language in any form because computer understands these signals directly. But, Assembly language needs to be converted in equivalent Binary code, so that computer can understand the instructions written in Assembly. Assembler is used to convert an assembly code to its equivalent Binary code.

The codes written in such kind of languages are difficult to write, read, edit and understand; the programs are not portable to any other computer system.

Low Level programming language programs are faster than High Level programming language programs as they have less keyword, symbols and no need (less need) to convert into Machine Code.

High Level Programming Languages

These are the machine independent programming languages, which are easy to write, read, edit and understand.

The languages like Java, .Net, Pascal, COBOL, C++, C, C# and other (which are very popular now to develop user end applications). These languages come under the high level programming language category.

High level programming languages have some special keywords, functions and class libraries by using them we can easily build a program for the computer.

Computer does not understand program written in such languages directly, as written above that computer understands only Machine code. So, here programming translators are required to convert a high level program to its equivalent Machine code.

Programming translators such as Compilers and Interpreters are the system software's which converts a program written in particular programming languages to its equivalent Machine code.

Here are the features of High Level programming languages:

- The programs are written in High Level programming languages and are independent that means a program written on a system can be run on another system.

- Easy to understand - Since these programming languages have keywords, functions, class libraries (which are similar to English words) we can easily understand the meaning of particular term related to that programming language.

- Easy to code, read and edit - The programs written in High Level programming languages are easy to code, read and edit. Even we can edit programs written by other programmers easily by having little knowledge of that programming language.

- Since, High Level language programs are slower than Low level language programs; still these programming languages are popular to develop User End Applications.

Middle Level Programming Language

Since, there is no such category of computer programming languages, but the programming languages that have features of low level and high level programming languages come under this category.

Hence, we can say that the programming languages which have features of Low Level as well as High Level programming languages known as "Middle Level" programming language.

C programming languages is the best example of Low Level Programming languages as it has features of low level and high level programming languages both.

References

- What-is-component-diagram, modeling-language: visual-paradigm.com, Retrieved 15 May, 2019

- Software-engineering-data-flow-diagrams: javatpoint.com, Retrieved 19 July, 2019

- Design-patterns-set-1-introduction: geeksforgeeks.org, Retrieved 9 March, 2019

- Creational-patterns: sourcemaking.com, Retrieved 21 January, 2019

- Design-patterns-set-2-factory-method: geeksforgeeks.org, Retrieved 10 April, 2019

- Creational-design-patterns-builder-pattern: dzone.com, Retrieved 18 August, 2019

- Abstract-factory-pattern: tutorialspoint.com, Retrieved 8 May, 2019

- Structural-patterns, design-patterns: sourcemaking.com, Retrieved 20 July, 2019

- Adapter-pattern: geeksforgeeks.org, Retrieved 3 June, 2019

- Proxy-pattern: tutorialspoint.com, Retrieved 13 February, 2019

- Behavioural-design-patterns-command: dzone.com, Retrieved 17 August, 2019

- Iterator-design-pattern: opencodez.com, Retrieved 7 June, 2019

- Computer-programming-languages: includehelp.com, Retrieved 22 April, 2019

Software User Interface Design and Construction

The design of different types of software interfaces which enable the users to interact with the computers is software user interface design. Graphical user interface is a common type of user interface. The chapter closely examines the key concepts of software user interface design and construction to provide an extensive understanding of the subject.

User interface (UI) design is the process of making interfaces in software or computerized devices with a focus on looks or style. Designers aim to create designs users will find easy to use and pleasurable. UI design typically refers to graphical user interfaces but also includes others, such as voice-controlled ones.

Designing UIs for User Delight

User interfaces are the access points where users interact with designs. Graphical user interfaces (GUIs) are designs' control panels and faces; voice-controlled interfaces involve oral-auditory interaction, while gesture-based interfaces witness users engaging with 3D design spaces via bodily motions. User interface design is a craft that involves building an essential part of the user experience; users are very swift to judge designs on usability and likeability. Designers focus on building interfaces users will find highly usable and efficient. Thus, a thorough understanding of the contexts users will find themselves in when making those judgments is crucial. You should create the illusion that users aren't interacting with a device so much as they're trying to attain goals directly and as effortlessly as possible. This is in line with the intangible nature of software – instead of depositing icons on a screen; you should aim to make the interface effectively invisible, offering users portals through which they can interact directly with the reality of their tasks. Focus on sustaining this "magic" by letting users find their way about the interface intuitively – the less they notice they must use controls, the more they'll immerse themselves. This dynamic applies to another dimension of UI design: Your design should have as many enjoyable features as are appropriate.

Facebook's easy-to-use layout affords instant brand recognition.

UI vs. UX Design

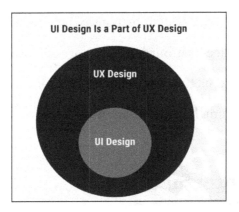

Often confused with UX design, UI design is more concerned with the surface and overall feel of a design, whereas the latter covers the entire spectrum of the user experience. One analogy is to picture UX design as a vehicle with UI design as the driving console. In GUIs, you should create pleasing aesthetics and animations that convey your organization's values and maximize usability.

"If we want users to like our software, we should design it to behave like a likeable person: respectful, generous and helpful."

How to make Great UIs

To deliver impressive GUIs, remember – users are humans, with needs such as comfort and low cognitive loads. Follow these guidelines:

1. Make elements such as buttons and other common elements perform predictably (including responses such as pinch = zoom) so users can unconsciously use them everywhere. Form should follow function.

2. Maintain high discoverability. Clearly label icons and include well-indicated affordances.

3. Keep interfaces simple and create an "invisible" feel. Every element must serve a purpose.

4. Respect the user's eye and attention regarding layout; focus on hierarchy and readability:

   - Alignment – minimize your number of alignment lines (think justified text); typically choose edge (over center) alignment.

   - Draw attention to key features using:

     ◦ Color, brightness and contrast. Avoid including colors or buttons excessively.

     ◦ Text via font sizes, bold type/weighting, italics, capitals and distance between letters. Users should pick up meanings just by scanning.

5. Minimize the number of actions for performing tasks but focus on one chief function per page; guide users by indicating preferred actions. Ease complex tasks by using progressive disclosure.

6. Put controls near objects users want to control.

7. Keep users informed vis-à-vis system responses/actions with feedback.

8. Consider defaults to reduce user burdens (e.g., pre-fill forms).

9. Use reusable design patterns to guide behavior regarding navigation and search functions.

10. Concentrate on maintaining brand consistency.

Graphical User Interface

The graphical user interface (GUI) heralded a new era for users' interaction with machines and computer systems. This innovation offered a new way for people to interact with systems in such a way that they didn't need to learn any coding principles. This killed off a previously steep learning curve for entry.

The GUI was designed first to make use of a keyboard and mouse, but today we see GUIs that take advantage of all manner of hardware inputs, as well as no hardware inputs at all. These interfaces have also made website-building a much easier task.

Blogging platforms like WordPress offer services that are almost entirely hinged on intuitive GUI systems to allow people to build websites without needing to learn any sort of scripting or coding. Previously, users needed to get to grips with a host of languages like HTML or CSS, or outsource to someone who had the necessary expertise.

The GUI has been connected with some of the biggest players in the industry, rather than being attributed to any single individual. Firms like Apple, however, were among the first to implement the GUI to its machines, namely the Lisa and Macintosh.

Since then, the GUI has evolved in leaps and bounds, transcending the keyboard and mouse configuration it was originally configured against. Experienced users sometimes prefer a command line interface because, when used properly, computing processes can be streamlined and made much quicker. GUIs also demand more memory and processing power, but with modern computing technology and software optimisations, it's not going to be the first thing you strip away in order to get a performance boost from your PC.

Benefits of a Graphical User Interface

The major benefit of a GUI is that systems using one are accessible to people of all levels of knowledge, from an absolute beginner to an advanced developer or other tech-savvy individuals. They make it simple for anyone to open menus, move files, launch programs or search the internet without having to tell the computer via the command line to carry out a function.

GUIs also provide instant feedback. Clicking an icon will open it up, for example, and this can be seen in real-time. Using a command line interface, you won't know whether it's a valid entry until you hit return; if it's not valid, nothing will happen.

Disadvantages of using a Graphical User Interface

Because the elements are graphics rather than text, GUIs can use a lot more processing power compared to a standard text-based UI.

Additionally, advanced users can find GUIs frustrating, because often a chain of actions will have to happen (such as opening up a menu, navigating to the file you want to open, clicking it) before the process is complete. With a text or command-line UI, one single line can be inputted and it will be actioned.

Graphic Control Elements

Graphical User Interface makes use of visual elements mostly. These elements define the appearance of the GUI. Some of these are described in detail as follows:

Window

This is the element that displays the information on the screen. It is very easy to manipulate a window. It can be opened or closed with the click of an icon. Moreover, it can be moved to any area by dragging it around. In a multitasking environment, multiple windows can be open at the same time, all of them performing different tasks.

There are multiple types of windows in a graphical user interface, such as container window, browser window, text terminal window, child window, message window etc.

Menu

A menu contains a list a choices and it allows users to select one from them. A menu bar is displayed horizontally across the screen such as pull down menu. When any option is clicked in this menu, then the pull down menu appears.

Another type of menu is the context menu that appears only when the user performs a specific action. An example of this is pressing the right mouse button. When this is done, a menu will appear under the cursor.

Icons

Files, programs, web pages etc. can be represented using a small picture in a graphical user interface. This picture is known as an icon. Using an icon is a fast way to open documents, run programs etc. because clicking on them yields instant access.

Controls

Information in an application can be directly read or influences using the graphical control elements. These are also known as widgets. Normally, widgets are used to display lists of similar items, navigate the system using links, tabs etc. and manipulating data using check boxes, radio boxes etc.

Tabs

A tab is associated with a view pane. It usually contains a text label or a graphical icon. Tabs are sometimes related to widgets and multiple tabs allow users to switch between different widgets. Tabs are used in various web browsers such as Internet Explorer, Firefox, Opera, Safari etc. Multiple web pages can be opened in a web browser and users can switch between them using tabs.

Hyper Text Markup Language

HTML (Hypertext Markup Language) is a text-based approach to describing how content contained within an HTML file is structured. This markup tells a web browser how to display text, images and other forms of multimedia on a webpage.

HTML is a formal recommendation by the World Wide Web Consortium (W3C) and is generally adhered to by all major web browsers, including both desktop and mobile web browsers. HTML5 is the latest version of the specification.

Basics of an HTML Element

Using HTML, a document containing text is further marked up with additional text describing how the document should be displayed. To keep the markup part separate from the actual content of the HTML file, there is a special, distinguishing HTML syntax that is used. These special components are known as HTML tags. The tags can contain name-value pairs known as attributes, and a piece of content that is enclosed within a tag is referred to as an HTML element.

An HTML element always has an opening tag, content in the middle and a closing tag. Attributes can provide additional information about the element and are included in the opening tag. Elements can be described in one of two ways:

1. Block-level elements start on a new line in the document and take up their own space. Examples of these elements include headings and paragraph tags.

2. Inline elements do not start on a new line in the document and only take up necessary space. These elements usually format the contents of block-level elements. Examples of inline elements include hyperlinks and text format tags.

Commonly used HTML Tags

The role of HTML is to inform a web browser about how the content contained within an HTML file is structured. Commonly used HTML tags include:

- <H1> which describes a top-level heading.

- <H2> which describes a second-level heading.

- <p> which describes a paragraph.

- <table> which describes tabular data.

- <ol> which describes an ordered list of information.

As you can see from this very short list, HTML tags primarily dictate the structural elements of a page.

Use and Implement of HTML

Because HTML is completely text-based, an HTML file can be edited simply by opening it up in a program such as Notepad++, Vi or Emacs. Any text editor can be used to create or edit an HTML file and, so long as the file is created with an .html extension, any web browser, such as Chrome or Firefox, will be capable of displaying the file as a webpage.

For professional software developers, there are a variety of WYSIWYG editors to develop webpages. NetBeans, IntelliJ, Eclipse and Microsoft's Visual Studio provide WYSIWYG editors as either plug-ins or as standard components, making it incredibly easy to use and implement HTML.

These WYSIWYG editors also provide HTML troubleshooting facilities, although modern web browsers often contain web developer plug-ins that will highlight problems with HTML pages, such as a missing end tag or syntax that does not create well-formed HTML.

Chrome and Firefox both include HTML developer tools that allow for the immediate viewing of a webpage's complete HTML file, along with the ability to edit HTML on the fly and immediately incorporate changes within the browser.

HTML, CSS and JavaScript

HTML is used to create web pages, but does experience limitations when it comes to fully responsive components. Therefore, HTML should only be used to add text elements and structure them within a page. For more complex features, HTML can be combined with cascading style sheets (CSS) and JavaScript (JS).

An HTML file can link to a cascading style sheet or JS file, which will contain information about which colors to use, which fonts to use and other HTML element rendering information. JavaScript also allows developers to include more dynamic functionality, such as pop-ups and photo sliders, in a web page.

Separating information about how a page is structured, which is the role of HTML, from the information about how a webpage looks when it is rendered in a browser is a software development pattern and best practice known as separation of concerns.

New Features of HTML5

In the early days of the World Wide Web, marking up text-based documents using HTML syntax was more than sufficient to facilitate the sharing of academic documents and technical memos. However, as the internet expanded beyond the walls of academia and into the homes of the general population, greater demand was placed on webpages in terms of formatting and interactivity.

HTML 4.01 was released in 1999, at a time when the internet was not yet a household name, and

HTML5 was not standardized until 2014. During this time, HTML markup drifted from the job of simply describing the structure of the content on a webpage into the role of also describing how content should look when a webpage displays it.

As a result, HTML4-based webpages often included information within a tag about what font to use when displaying text, what color should be used for the background and how content should be aligned. Describing within an HTML tag how an HTML element should be formatted when rendered on a webpage is considered an HTML antipattern. HTML should describe how content is structured, not how it will be styled and rendered within a browser.

The separation of concerns pattern is more rigorously enforced in HTML5 than it was in HTML4. With HTML5, the bold <b> and italicize <i> tags have been deprecated. For the paragraph tag, the align attribute has been completely removed from the HTML specification.

For the purpose of backward-compatibility, web browsers will continue to support these deprecated HTML tags, but the changes to the HTML specification do demonstrate the desire of the community for HTML to return to its original purpose of describing the structure of content, while encouraging developers to use cascading style sheets for formatting purposes.

Another important feature of HTML5 when compared to HTML4 is the support of audio and video embedding. Instead of using plugins, multimedia can be placed within the HTML code using an <audio> or <video> tag. Additionally, there is built-in support for scalable vector graphics and MathML for mathematical and scientific formulas.

Editing HTML Example

In the following HTML example, there are two HTML elements. Both elements use the same paragraph tag, designated with the letter p, and both use the directional attribute dir, although a different value is assigned to the HTML attribute's name-value pairing, namely rtl and ltr.

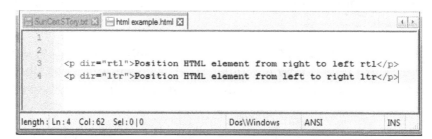

An example of an HTML element using the paragraph tag and the direction attribute dir.

Cascading Style Sheets

Cascading style sheets are used to format the layout of Web pages. They can be used to define text styles, table sizes, and other aspects of Web pages that previously could only be defined in a page's HTML.

CSS helps Web developers create a uniform look across several pages of a Web site. Instead of defining the style of each table and each block of text within a page's HTML, commonly used styles need to be defined only once in a CSS document. Once the style is defined in cascading style sheet, it can be used by any page that references the CSS file. Plus, CSS makes it easy to change styles across several pages at once. For example, a Web developer may want to increase the default text size from 10pt to 12pt for fifty pages of a Web site. If the pages all reference the same style sheet, the text size only needs to be changed on the style sheet and all the pages will show the larger text.

While CSS is great for creating text styles, it is helpful for formatting other aspects of Web page layout as well. For example, CSS can be used to define the cell padding of table cells, the style, thickness, and color of a table's border, and the padding around images or other objects. CSS gives Web developers more exact control over how Web pages will look than HTML does. This is why most Web pages today incorporate cascading style sheets.

Advantages of CSS

- CSS saves time: You can write CSS once and then reuse same sheet in multiple HTML pages. You can define a style for each HTML element and apply it to as many Web pages as you want.

- Pages load faster: If you are using CSS, you do not need to write HTML tag attributes every time. Just write one CSS rule of a tag and apply it to all the occurrences of that tag. So less code means faster download times.

- Easy maintenance: To make a global change, simply change the style, and all elements in all the web pages will be updated automatically.

- Superior styles to HTML: CSS has a much wider array of attributes than HTML, so you can give a far better look to your HTML page in comparison to HTML attributes.

- Multiple Device Compatibility: Style sheets allow content to be optimized for more than one type of device. By using the same HTML document, different versions of a website can be presented for handheld devices such as PDAs and cell phones or for printing.

- Global web standards: Now HTML attributes are being deprecated and it is being recommended to use CSS. So it's a good idea to start using CSS in all the HTML pages to make them compatible to future browsers.

Who Creates and Maintains CSS?

CSS is created and maintained through a group of people within the W3C called the CSS Working Group. The CSS Working Group creates documents called specifications. When a specification has been discussed and officially ratified by the W3C members, it becomes a recommendation.

These ratified specifications are called recommendations because the W3C has no control over the actual implementation of the language. Independent companies and organizations create that software.

The World Wide Web Consortium or W3C is a group that makes recommendations about how the Internet works and how it should evolve.

Client-Side Scripting

In web applications, there is the server and the client (user). The "server" is a web application server at a remote area that will execute web requests & send pages to the client. Whereas the "client" refers to a web browser, such as Firefox, Chrome, Google, etc. Web applications can contain code that is handled on the user's (client's) browser or on the web server. On the other hand, web applications have a separated architecture, which implies that there is never a live, constant connection between the page showed in the user's (client's) browser and database server or a web. Most of the processing will be carried out at the server and not on the client's web browser. At the point when a database needs to be approached on a server, the web application will present the page once again on the web server and server-side code will process the request.

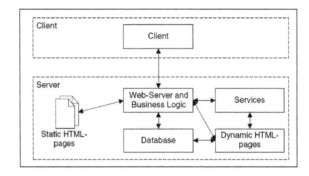

Server side scripting is a technique used in website designing to create dynamic web pages based various conditions when the user's (client's) browser makes a request to the server. The Web Server executes the server side scripting which produces the page to be send to the browser. Server executes server-side scripts to forward a page however it doesn't execute client-side scripts.

The Server side scripting is often used to connect with the databases that locate on the web server. Also it can approach the file system lying at the web server. It is generally observed that response from a server-side script is slower when compared to a client-side script as the scripts are prepared on the seclude computer. PHP, Python, Ruby are some common examples of server-side scripting.

Examples of Server-side Scripting

- PHP
- ASP
- JSP
- Python
- Pearl
- Ruby
- Node.js
- Cold Fusion Markup Language- CFML

Benefits of Server-side Scripting

- Server-side Scripting doesn't require the client's (user's) to download plugins such as Flash or JavaScript.

- Scripts are usually hidden from the views. Only HTML output can be view by the users, even if they view the source.

Drawbacks of Server-side Scripting

The scripts can be utilized by hackers to get access to the server. Since the scripts react to URL info, altering the URL to something that endeavors a security hole & can give the client server access, here and there even as root.

Cient-side Scripting

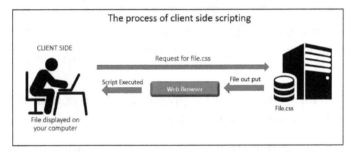

Client Side Scripting is utilized when the client's (user's) browser has all the code and the page is modified on the basis of the client's (user's) information. The Web Browser executes the client side scripting that locates within the user's computer. Client-side scripts are also known as embedded script (as they are often embedded within an HTML or XHTML document).

The browser gets the page sent by the server & executes the client-side scripts. Client side scripting can't be utilized to join with the databases on the web server. Client side scripting cannot get the file system which lies at the web server.

The records and settings which are local at the client's (user's) computer can be approached employing Client side scripting language. It's generally observed the response from a client-side script is faster when compared to a server-side scripting language as the scripts are prepared on the local computers. JavaScript, VB scripts are some common example of client-side scripting.

Examples of Popular Client-side Scriptings

- JavaScript

- ActionScript

- VBScript (can be used on serverside also)

- Dart

- TypeScript

- Python

Advantages of Client-Side Scripting

- Client-side Scripting offers faster response times, less overhead on the web server and a more interactive application.

- Ideal for altering the page elements without the need to contact the database.

Disadvantages of Client-Side Scripting

The drawback of client-side scripting is that the scripting language calls for more effort and time, while the user's browser must support the scripting language also.

Asynchronous JavaScript and XML

AJAX stands for Asynchronous JavaScript and XML. AJAX is a new technique for creating better, faster, and more interactive web applications with the help of XML, HTML, CSS, and Java Script.

- Ajax uses XHTML for content, CSS for presentation, along with Document Object Model and JavaScript for dynamic content display.

- Conventional web applications transmit information to and from the sever using synchronous requests. It means you fill out a form, hit submit, and get directed to a new page with new information from the server.

- With AJAX, when you hit submit, JavaScript will make a request to the server, interpret the results, and update the current screen. In the purest sense, the user would never know that anything was even transmitted to the server.

- XML is commonly used as the format for receiving server data, although any format, including plain text, can be used.

- AJAX is a web browser technology independent of web server software.

- A user can continue to use the application while the client program requests information from the server in the background.

- Intuitive and natural user interaction. Clicking is not required; mouse movement is a sufficient event trigger.

- Data-driven as opposed to page-driven.

Rich Internet Application Technology

AJAX is the most viable Rich Internet Application (RIA) technology so far. It is getting tremendous industry momentum and several tool kit and frameworks are emerging. But at the same time, AJAX has browser incompatibility and it is supported by JavaScript, which is hard to maintain and debug.

AJAX is based on Open Standards

AJAX is based on the following open standards:

- Browser-based presentation using HTML and Cascading Style Sheets (CSS).

- Data is stored in XML format and fetched from the server.

- Behind-the-scenes data fetches using XMLHttpRequest objects in the browser.

- JavaScript to make everything happen.

Simple (Model–View) User Interface

The development of user interfaces (UIs), ranging from early requirements to software obsolescence, has become a time-consuming and costly process. Typically, the graphical user interface (GUI) of an interactive system represents about 48% of the source code, requires about 45% of the development time and 50% of the implementation time, and covers 37% of the maintenance time. These figures, evaluated in the early nineties, are increasing dramatically with the spread of new interaction techniques such as vocal and gestural modalities, resulting in additional requirements.

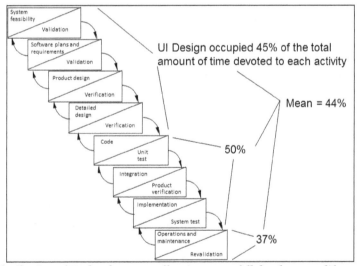

Distribution of UI development effort in a waterfall development life cycle.

Today, developers of UI for interactive systems have to address multiple sources of heterogeneity:

- Heterogeneity of end users: an interactive system is normally used by several different end users. End users differ with respect to their preferences, capabilities, culture (e.g., speaking different languages) and level of experience.

- Heterogeneity of computing platforms, interaction modalities, input/output capabilities: there is a large diversity of computing platforms (e.g., smartphone, desktop PC, tablet, embedded devices) using different input capabilities (e.g., keyboard, mouse, (multi-)touch, data gloves, motion sensors, monitors, head-mounted displays) with different interaction modalities (e.g., graphics, speech, haptics, gesture, Brain-Computer-Interaction).

- Heterogeneity of programming/markup languages and widget toolkits: for developing a UI, developers use different programming/markup languages (e.g., Java, C++, HTML) with different widget libraries (e.g., Swing, Qt, GTK+).

- Heterogeneity of working environments: many workflows in the real world are supported by interactive systems through the pervasiveness of computing devices. As a result, developers have to consider different contextual constraints (e.g., noisy environments, mobility).

- Variability of the context of use (<user, platform, environment>). In addition to being heterogeneous, the context of use dynamically evolves, calling for plastic UIs, i.e. UIs capable of adaptation while preserving human values. The dimensions that characterize UI plasticity are presented in The Problem Space of UI adaptation, UI Plasticity.

Model-Based User Interface Development (MBUID) is one approach that aims at coping with the above mentioned challenges and at decreasing the effort needed to develop UIs while ensuring UI quality. The purpose of Model-Based Design is to identify high-level models that allow designers to specify and analyse interactive software applications from a more semantic oriented level rather than starting immediately to address the implementation level. This allows them to concentrate on more important aspects without being immediately confused by many implementation details and then to have tools which update the implementation in order to be consistent with high-level choices.

For a comprehensive overview of the history and evolution of MBUID, we refer to. Different frameworks have been developed to conceptually capture the important aspects of a MBUID process. As early as, Szekely introduced a generic architecture for MBUID In, Da Silva described architecture for UI development using a MBUID approach. The first version of a reference framework for multiple contexts of use UIs in history using a model-based approach appeared in. This version was then extended with additional relationships and definitions to give rise to a revised reference framework published for the first time in July and in. It was then named the Cameleon Reference Framework (CRF) when accepted as a new deliverable of the EU-funded FP 5 CAMELEON project, published in September. CRF has now become widely accepted in the HCI Engineering community as a reference for structuring and classifying model-based development processes of UIs that support multiple contexts of use. CRF covers both the design time and run time phases. In metamodels and the use of models at runtime are proposed for supporting UI plasticity.

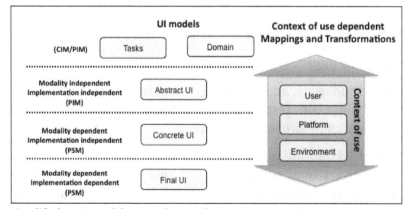

A simplified version of the Cameleon Reference Framework (CRF). Mappings and transformations between levels of abstraction depend on the context of use.

As depicted in figure, the CRF makes explicit a set of UI models (e.g., Tasks, Abstract UI, Concrete UI, and Final UI) and their relationships, to serve as a common vocabulary within the HCI Engineering community to discuss and express different perspectives on a UI.

- The Task and Domain models correspond to the hierarchies of tasks that need to be performed on/with domain objects (or domain concepts) in a specific temporal logical order for achieving users' goals (during the interaction with the UI). Using the wording of the OMG Model-Driven Architecture (MDA) in Software Engineering, the Task and Domain level is either a Computing Independent Model (CIM) or a Platform Independent Model (PIM).

- The Abstract UI (AUI) model expresses the UI in terms of Abstract Interaction Units (AIU) (or Abstract Interaction Objects (AIOs), as well as the relationships among them. These AIUs are independent of any implementation technology or modality (e.g., graphical, vocal, gestural). They can be grouped logically to map logically connected tasks or domain objects.

- The Concrete UI (CUI) model expresses the UI in terms of Concrete Interaction Units (CIU) (or Concrete Interaction Objects (CIOs). These CIUs are modality-dependent, but implementation technology independent, thus platform specific (PSM). The CUI concretely defines how the UI is perceived and can be manipulated by end users.

- The Final UI (FUI) model expresses the UI in terms of implementation technology dependent source code. A FUI can be represented in any UI programming language (e.g., Java UI toolkit) or mark-up language (e.g., HTML). A FUI can then be compiled or interpreted.

The relationships between the CRF models include concretization, abstraction, translation, and reflexion.

- Concretization is an operation that transforms a particular model into another one of a lower level of abstraction, until executable/interpretable code is reached. CRF shows a four-step concretization process: the Task and Domain level (task model and/or the domain model) is "concretized" into an Abstract UI model, which in turn leads to a Concrete UI. A Concrete UI is then turned into a Final UI, typically by means of code generation techniques.

- Abstraction is an operation that transforms a UI representation from any level of abstraction to a higher level of abstraction. Reverse engineering of user interfaces is a typical example of abstraction.

- Translation is an operation that transforms a description intended for a particular context of use into a description at the same level of abstraction, but aimed at a different context of use.

- Reflexion is an operation that transforms a model into another one at the same level of abstraction for the same context of use (as opposed to different contexts of use as for translation).

The aforementioned relationships always preserve some dimension, either vertically (i.e., concretization and abstraction) or horizontally (i.e., translation, reflexion). In order to address non-horizontal/vertical transformations, Cross-cutting is a transformation of a model into another one at a different level of abstraction (higher or lower), while changing the context of use.

Orthogonal to the Task-Domain, AUI, CUI and FUI models, CRF makes explicit the context of use that may have an impact on the nature of the transformations used in the transformation process. The term "context of use" denotes an information space structured into three main models:

- The user model includes attributes and functions that describe the archetypal person who is intended to use, or is actually using, the interactive system (e.g., profile, idiosyncrasies, current tasks and activities).

- The platform model includes an integrated collection of software and hardware technologies and resource specifications that bind together the physical environment with the digital world.

- The environment model includes spatio-temporal attributes, rules, and functions that characterize the physical and social places when/where the interaction will take place, or is actually taking place. This includes numeric and/or symbolic times and locations (e.g., in the morning, at 4 o'clock, at home, in a public space, on the move in the street, in the train or car), light and sound conditions, social rules and activities (e.g., hierarchical social organization, roles, spatial and temporal relationships).

Although context of use is mainly defined based on information about users, platforms, and environments, there are also other dimensions that can be relevant to characterize context and to properly adapt an interactive system. The application domain, for instance, can also add relevant information that completes the characteristics of the context of use. For example, in a safety critical environment, knowing that the interactive system supports air traffic control or a nuclear power plant provides useful information about the level of attention that is required from end users.

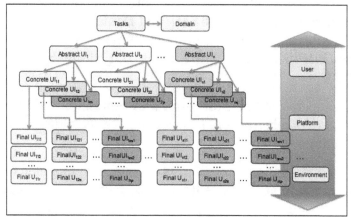

One example of possible transformations across the levels of CRF according to different contexts of use, starting from a unique Task and Domain Model.

Unlike the process initiated in the 1980s, which contained one entry point only at a high level of abstraction, CRF enables entry and exit points at any level of abstraction from which any combination of horizontal and vertical bottom-up and top-down transformations can be applied. This theoretical flexibility means that the stakeholders involved in the development of an interactive system can use the development process that best suits their practice or the case at hand. Even when using a top down approach, developers can explore multiple development paths in parallel as illustrated in Figure. However, due to this high flexibility, developers have to ensure that models are not manipulated "by hand" after a transformation has been done. If so, developers have to ensure model consistency by e.g., using reverse transformations from a more concrete level to a more abstract level.

Benefits from using Model based UI Development

This section provides a list of potential benefits that are usually discussed for model-based development and Model-Driven Engineering (MDE) in general. Each potential benefit is then refined in the context of UI development. General MDE benefits are reported in:

1. Benefits resulting from the existence of a step-wise development life cycle:

- Reducing the gap between requirements and implementation: a modelling phase aims to ensure in advance that the implementation addresses the user-centered requirements. MBUID contributes to this by explicitly defining models related to the UI that are captured and updated throughout the development life cycle. The output of a development step could serve as an input for a next development step. Among typical models is the task model, the domain model, the context of use model, thus promoting a user-centered development life cycle. These models are often, but not always, specified according to declarative programming, a programming paradigm in which the logic of the UI is described without describing its control flow. Other programming paradigms (e.g., logic programming, functional programming, imperative/procedural programming) are also used individually or mixed together.

- Coordinating the involvement of multiple stakeholders: previous planning of the development life cycle enables various stakeholders (e.g., project leaders, designers, developers, testers, end users, psychologists, marketing people) to coordinate their work, e.g., by dividing the interactive system into several parts and defining mappings between them. Separation of concerns supports capturing various UI aspects in independent, but possibly correlated, models thus enabling these different stakeholders to fulfill their respective roles.

- Producing well-structured systems: the stepwise development life cycle together with the separation of concerns provide a good basis for producing a well-structured system, thus facilitating implementation itself as well as maintenance.

2. Benefits resulting from the use of explicit abstract models:

- Planning an adequate level of abstraction: Modeling languages provide the developer with concepts for planning and reasoning about the developed system at the appropriate level of abstraction. MBUID contributes to this benefit by defining the levels of abstraction described in CRF.

- Improving communication by explicit models: The explicitness of modeling languages, in particular their visual representation, can lead to increased quality (e.g., understanding, perceiving, exploring, explaining, justifying, comparing, etc.,) of design documents for all stakeholders. For instance, MBUID contributes to this benefit by explicitly defining semantics, syntax, and stylistics for each model.

- Supporting UI quality: (Semi-) Formal modeling languages explicitly support UI compliance with respect to requirements (e.g., UI quality factors, usability guidelines, accessibility guidelines (e.g., WCAG), validation rules for completeness, consistency, correctness).

3. Benefits from exploring alternative designs:

- Supporting creation & creativity: MBUID efficiently produces alternative models with different design options, parameters, thus fostering the exploration of the design space.

- Enabling the production and comparison of alternative designs for multiple contexts of use while preserving quality (e.g., consistency): When UIs need to be produced for multiple contexts of use, MBUID facilitates the rapid production and comparison of alternative designs (e.g., factoring out common parts that are context-independent from specific context-dependent parts), which is particularly useful in change management.

4. Benefits resulting from code generation: the benefits associated with this appear when the method is enacted.

- Enhancing development productivity: Code generation from a set of models often requires only a small fraction of time compared to the manual production of code. Consequently, MBUID favors UI rapid, iterative, agile development, including UI mockups and prototypes at different levels of fidelity.

- Capturing and reusing expert knowledge throughout UI development life cycle: Expert knowledge – e.g., about user interface design, usability engineering, code structuring, code optimizations, or platform-specific vs platform-independent features – once incorporated in various development steps, expert knowledge can then be reused by all stakeholders (especially developers and designers).

- Reducing errors: Automatic transformation avoids manual errors. "Integranova creates customised solutions in half the time, personalised solutions for half the price, and top-quality, error-free software.

5. Benefits from using models at runtime:

- Considering contexts of use that were not envisioned at design time: When a new context of use needs to be considered (e.g., opportunistic end user's needs), then models can be exploited at runtime to support on the fly adaptation.

- Explaining and justifying the UI to the end user: The UI is able to explain and to justify itself to the end user thanks to the models that capture the design rationale and that are embedded at runtime.

- Going beyond low level adaptation: Adaptation can span from the highest level of abstraction (e.g., the task and the domain models) to the lowest level (e.g., the final UI).

- Enabling UI evolution: When requirements continuously evolve at run time, the UI should be repeatedly modified, and so do its models, as well as the design knowledge used to produce it. This evolution could be governed by the user (i.e., manually by the way of a meta-user interface y the system (i.e., autonomously as in autonomic computing or by both (i.e., mixed-initiative.

6. Benefits for supporting method engineering:

- Defining and enacting method for UI development process: Once defined, a method could be enacted and any deviation with respect to the definition could be pointed out.

- Knowledge about creation of modeling languages: MDE concepts and definitions reflect existing knowledge about modeling, modeling languages, and code generation. MBUID contributes to this benefit by bringing expertise about models for user interface development.

- Usage of frameworks and tools: Various software tools, such as Integrated Development Environments (IDEs), could support MBUID. In more advanced model-driven engineering of UIs, tools exist that support MDE steps, such as creating and processing metamodels, creating modeling editors, and defining and executing transformations (e.g., transformation engines).

7. Maintenance of modeling language and transformations:

- Systematic and explicit definition of metamodels and transformations: When all models and transformations are defined according to a common set of meta-models, their usage becomes systematic. This also works for MBUID.

- Maintenance of modeling languages and code generators: Modeling languages, associated model-to-model transformations and model-to-code compilation can be maintained at a level of expressiveness that is higher than a traditional programming or markup language.

- Reuse of models, metamodels, and transformations: MDE compliant metamodels and transformations can be understood and reused by others. Models or model fragments could be reused from one use case to another or from one context of use to another, only affecting the portion that is subject to change. This reuse facilitates the development of plastic user interfaces.

Use Cases for Model-based UI Design

This section provides a list of implemented use cases to illustrate different CRF-compliant development processes. Table provides a synthetic view of the differentiating characteristics of these exemplars where lines refer to the level of abstraction used as the entry point from which transformations are performed, and where columns indicate whether these transformations are performed at design time or at run time.

Entry Point / Software Life Cycle Phase	Design Time	Run Time
Task & Domain	UC1 - Car Rental UC2 - Digital Home	UC3 - Minimalistic UIs
Abstract UI	UC4 Story Editor	UC5 - Post WIMP Widgets
Concrete UI	UC6 - Automotive Industry (Infotainment system design)	UC7- Photo-Browser
Final UI		UC8 - Tourism Web Site (TWS)

The car rental example consists of a scenario in which the interactive system permits users to rent a car. In this sense, various contextual information can be used to adapt application aspects, and to properly display the list of cars to rent, enabling users to make choices and to accomplish the main task.

The key functional requirements to support this task include the capacity to:

- Specify the pick-up and return locations of the car;
- Specify the period for the car rental;
- Access a set of possible cars and select one;
- Access and select additional car features (e.g. Gps);
- Provide personal information before renting the car;
- Access details about the car rental before making the final decision.

Two contexts of use are targeted:

- Context 1: Physical environment is that of a home, platform is a Desktop PC, and the user is an English speaker who does not know the city where the car has to be rented.
- Context 2: Physical environment is a busy street, platform is a smartphone, and the user is walking fast (busy eyes).

Figure illustrates how a MBUI approach can be applied using successive concretization transformations starting from a single Task and Domain Model to different Abstract User Interfaces (each one corresponding to a specific context of use) and iteratively down to Final User Interfaces.

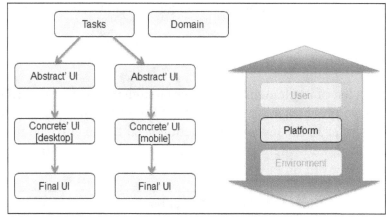

Models involved in the car rental use case and the process.

Digital Home

Responsible: CNR-ISTI.

Digital home refers to a residence with devices that are connected through a computer network. A digital home has a network of consumer electronics, mobile, and PC devices that cooperate transparently. All computing devices and home appliances conform to a set of interoperable standards so that everything can be controlled by means of an interactive system. Different electronic services can be offered by a digital home system, including but not limited to e.g., manage, synchronize and store personal content, family calendars and files; upload, play and show music, videos and pictures on a home screen (e.g., a TV) using a mobile phone as a remote control; use a mobile phone as a remote control for the other devices, for example a thermostat.

These functionalities are made available through context sensitive user interfaces. In fact, such UIs are capable of adapting to different computing platforms (touch-based devices, web, mobile, TV, PDA, DECT handset, voice portal, etc.), users (children, teenagers, adults, elderly, disabled people, etc.) and environments or situations (at home, away, at night, while music is playing, etc.). The final aim is to provide a seamless and unified user experience, which is critical in the digital home domain. To this regard, different automatic UI adaptations can be possible: e.g., zooming the UI if the user has visual problems; enabling multimodal interactions (ex. voice interaction) because the user is doing another task at the same time.

The key functional requirements for this application are the following:

- Authenticate a user in order to enable remote access to home devices,

- Select a room,

- Select a device inside the room,

- Inspect and modify the status of a selected device.

This application may be used in different contexts of use:

- Context 1: Physical environment is that of a home, platform is a Desktop PC, and the user controls the home devices without accessing directly the physical controls.

- Context 2: Physical environment is a street, and the user is moving. The user controls the home devices remotely, in order to e.g. start heating the home before coming back.

In this use case, the context dimension considered is limited to the platform aspect.

Figure show screenshots of the Digital Home for two targeted contexts of use.

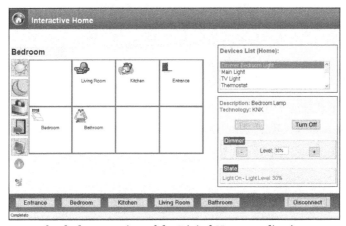

The desktop version of the Digital Home application.

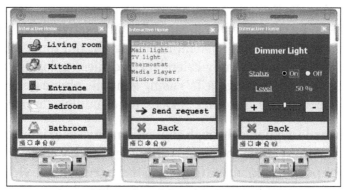

The mobile version of the Digital Home application.

The models involved in the Digital Home use case as well as the process involving them are depicted in figure.

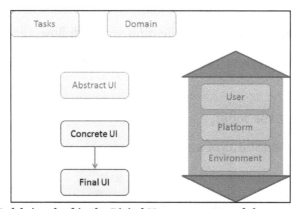

Models involved in the Digital Home use case and the process.

The use case considered in the Digital Home exemplar starts from the task model. Because we consider the platform as the only dimension of the context of use, the other context aspects have been greyed out in figure. From the task model, it is possible to derive an Abstract UI for each targeted context of use. Let's consider a desktop PC. On the one hand, this AUI will be expressed using a modality and platform -independent vocabulary (also shared by other AUIs addressing different computing platforms), on the other hand, this AUI will include only the abstract interaction units that make sense in that considered computing platform (a desktop PC). From this AUI, it is possible to obtain a Concrete UI and then a Final UI in a specific implementation language suitable for that computing platform. A similar process is followed to obtain a Final UI for a different platform (e.g., the mobile one). From the filtered CTT task model, an Abstract UI is derived and then a CUI and finally an implemented UI expressed in a language supported by the mobile platform is built.

- Omitting minimalistic UIs through the use of an universal interaction device in production environments. Responsible:
  - Heilbronn University (Gerrit Meixner)
  - DFKI (Marc Seissler)

The Smart Factory KL is an arbitrarily modifiable and expandable (flexible) intelligent production environment, connecting components from multiple manufacturers (networked), enabling its components to perform context-related tasks autonomously (self-organizing), and emphasizing user-friendliness (user-oriented). The Smart Factory KL is the first ambient intelligent production environment for demonstration and development purposes worldwide. Development of user interfaces is a secondary field in the production industry, but the impact of user interface quality is increasingly independent of the application domain, which is a significant factor of success for the entire product. After three years of research, a first prototype has been finished that allows for controlling the production line using a single universal interaction device able to adapt to varying field devices according to the actual context of use, in a complex, model-based approach. To handle the resulting diversity of user interfaces, we developed a universal interaction device – the SmartMote – which is capable of providing control over various devices in these environments. Depending on the context of use, the visualization of the SmartMote is generated and adapted during run-time in order to provide a homogeneous intra-device user experience.

The Smart Factory KL.

The key functional requirements for this application are the following:

- Authenticate a user in order to enable remote access to modules or field devices,

- Select a module or a field device,

- Inspect and interact (e.g. modify parameters) with a selected module or field device.

The SmartMote may be used in one context:

- Context 1: Physical environment is that of a production environment (industrial factory), platform is a tablet PC (+ modules or field devices from different vendors), one single user.

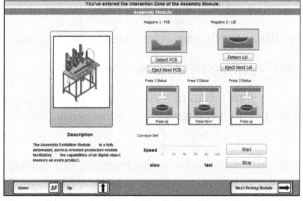

Screenshot of a rendered (final) UI with the SmartMote.

For the specification of the context-sensitive UI a model-based architecture has been developed that consists of two core models (AUI-model and CUI-model). The AUI-model is specified using the "Useware Dialog Modeling" Language (useDM) that enables the abstract, modality-independent specification of the user interface. This model is refined via a CUI-model that uses the User Interface Markup Language (UIML) 4.0 for the platform-independent description of the graphical user interface. Adaptation rules are further used to specify the adaptation that can be applied on those models at run-time. To generate the final user interface (FUI) a java-based Renderer – SmartMote – has been developed.

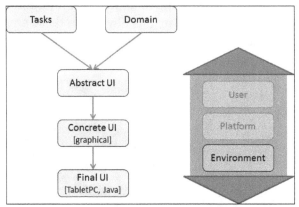

Models involved in the Minimalist-UI use case and the process.

Story Editor

The production of e-learning tools for deaf people meets with several difficulties, connected to the need to resort only to the visual channel, without saturating it, and to the adoption of different cognitive strategies developed within the community. From a field study conducted with deaf people in the context of a national project involving cognitive scientists, linguists, and computer scientists, we adopted the metaphor of a learning story as the basis for organising different types of learning material: videos, pictures, texts, accompanied by translation in the Italian Sign Language. We report on the use of a user interface abstract model in the development of the interactive story editor, to be used by tutors and teachers to organise the course material and path, and which generates interactive pages for the students.

The key functional requirements to support developers of course include:

- Specify the activities involved in a learning module;

- Specify the logical paths according to which these activities can be performed;

- Specify the conditions for progressing along these paths.

The context of use is that of the generation of a course by a teacher, possibly involving in the process tutors who will then have to assist the learners. Learners and tutors will then interact with the generated web pages.

The development relies on an abstract model of the learning domain, in which stories are seen as workflows: (learning) processes in which tasks are assigned to actors (e.g., students and tutors). Stories can be recursively composed by sub-stories, paths define sequences or alternatives for exploration of stories, with transitions connecting sub-stories, and tasks either are defined as simple stories to be explored individually or in a laboratory, or require the exploration of sub-stories. Each story has a single entry point and a single exit point, signalling completion by the student.

Stories are classified with respect to the exploration strategy and associated with abstract patterns. For example, in a star topology tasks can be performed in any order. For each type, the story editor provides a specialised form of interaction, guiding the teacher to define the story according to that type, and a template is used to generate the appropriate main page for the story accordingly.

The models involved in the Digital Home use case as well as the process involving them are depicted in figure.

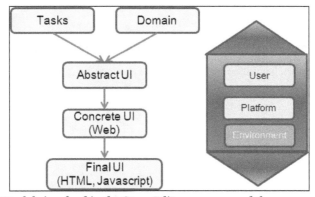

Models involved in the Story Editor use case and the process.

The design of the interaction with the Story Editor and of the templates for the generated pages derives from the representation of tasks in the form of patterns composed by specific task trees. For each pattern, the story editor will constrain the interaction to create instances of that pattern, and will generate the specific workflow to be followed while interacting with the generated page. Moreover a corresponding pattern of interaction elements to be included in the generated page is provided as an abstract user interface model.

The target platform is that of Web pages with associated JavaScript components for the interaction with the specific learning content.

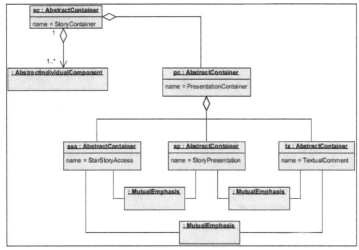

The overall abstract structure of story containers.

As shown in figure, a Story Container will present several individual components, providing context for the interaction, and a Presentation Container, composed of several different "page contents" in a mutual emphasis relation so that they cannot be shown together). The specific composition of the presentation container will depend on the type of story to be presented, as prescribed by the Task Model, where either an individual component or a container is associated with each task.

References

- What-is-a-graphical-user-interface, operating-systems: itpro.co.uk, Retrieved 27 March, 2019
- Graphical-user-interface-gui: tutorialspoint.com, Retrieved 3 May, 2019
- HTML-Hypertext-Markup-Language: theserverside.com, Retrieved 23 January, 2019
- What-is-css: tutorialspoint.com, Retrieved 28 April, 2019
- What-are-client-side-and-server-side-scripting-web: admecindia.co.in, Retrieved 8 June, 2019
- What_is_ajax, ajax: tutorialspoint.com, Retrieved 10 February, 2019

Software Testing: Verification and Validation

The investigation which is conducted for providing stakeholders with information about the quality of a software product or service is known software testing. The different types of software testing are primarily divided into functional testing and non-functional testing. This chapter discusses in detail the different types of software testing as well as levels of software testing.

Software testing is the process of evaluating and verifying that a software product or application does what it is supposed to do. The benefits of testing include preventing bugs, reducing development costs and improving performance.

Software testing arrived alongside the development of software, which had its beginnings just after the Second World War. Computer scientist Tom Kilburn is credited with writing the first piece of software, which debuted on June 21, 1948, at the University of Manchester in England. It performed mathematical calculations using machine code instructions.

Debugging was the main testing method at the time and remained so for the next two decades. By the 1980s, development teams looked beyond isolating and fixing software bugs to testing applications in real-world settings. It set the stage for a broader view of testing, which encompassed a quality assurance process that was part of the software development life cycle.

"In the 1990s, there was a transition from testing to a more comprehensive process called quality assurance, which covers the entire software development cycle and affects the processes of planning, design, creation and execution of test cases, support for existing test cases and test environments," says Alexander Yaroshko in his post on the uTest developer site.

"Testing had reached a qualitatively new level, which led to the further development of methodologies, the emergence of powerful tools for managing the testing process and test automation tools."

Continuous Testing

Software testing has traditionally been separated from the rest of development. It is often conducted later in the software development life cycle after the product build or execution stage. A tester may only have a small window to test the code – sometimes just before the application goes to market. If defects are found, there may be little time for recoding or retesting. It is not uncommon to release software on time, but with bugs and fixes needed. Or a testing team may fix errors but miss a release date.

Doing test activities earlier in the cycle helps keep the testing effort at the forefront rather than as an afterthought to development. Earlier software tests also mean that defects are less expensive to resolve.

Many development teams now use a methodology known as continuous testing. It is part of a DevOps approach – where development and operations collaborate over the entire product life cycle. The aim is to accelerate software delivery while balancing cost, quality and risk. With this testing technique, teams don't need to wait for the software to be built before testing starts. They can run tests much earlier in the cycle to discover defects sooner, when they are easier to fix.

Importance of Software Testing

Few can argue against the need for quality control when developing software. Late delivery or software defects can damage a brand's reputation — leading to frustrated and lost customers. In extreme cases, a bug or defect can degrade interconnected systems or cause serious malfunctions.

Consider Nissan having to recall over 1 million cars due to a software defect in the airbag sensor detectors. Or a software bug that caused the failure of a $1.2 billion military satellite launch. The numbers speak for themselves. Software failures in the US cost the economy $1.1 trillion in assets in 2016. What's more, they impacted 4.4 billion customers.

Though testing itself costs money, companies can save millions per year in development and support if they have a good testing technique and QA processes in place. Early software testing uncovers problems before a product goes to market. The sooner development teams receive test feedback, the sooner they can address issues such as:

- Architectural flaws

- Poor design decisions

- Invalid or incorrect functionality

- Security vulnerabilities

- Scalability issues

When development leaves ample room for testing, it improves software reliability and high-quality applications are delivered with few errors. A system that meets or even exceeds customer expectations leads to potentially more sales and greater market share.

Features of Effective Software Testing

Software testing follows a common process. Tasks or steps include defining the test environment, developing test cases, writing scripts, analysing test results and submitting defect reports.

Testing can be time-consuming. Manual testing or ad-hoc testing may be enough for small builds. However, for larger systems, tools are frequently used to automate tasks. Automated testing helps teams implement different scenarios, test differentiators (such as moving components into a cloud environment), and quickly get feedback on what works and what doesn't.

A good testing approach encompasses the application programming interface (API), user interface and system levels. As well, the more tests that are automated, and run early, the better. Some teams build in-house test automation tools. However, vendor solutions offer features that can streamline key test management tasks such as:

- Continuous testing: Project teams test each build as it becomes available. This type of software testing relies on test automation that is integrated with the deployment process. It enables software to be validated in realistic test environments earlier in the process – improving design and reducing risks.

- Configuration management: Organizations centrally maintain test assets and track what software builds to test. Teams gain access to assets such as code, requirements, design documents, models, test scripts and test results. Good systems include user authentication and audit trails to help teams meet compliance requirements with minimal administrative effort.

- Service virtualization: Testing environments may not be available, especially early in code development. Service virtualization simulates the services and systems that are missing or not yet completed, enabling teams to reduce dependencies and test sooner. They can reuse, deploy and change a configuration to test different scenarios without having to modify the original environment.

- Defect or bug tracking: Monitoring defects is important to both testing and development teams for measuring and improving quality. Automated tools allow teams to track defects, measure their scope and impact, and uncover related issues.

- Metrics and reporting: Reporting and analytics enable team members to share status, goals and test results. Advanced tools integrate project metrics and present results in a dashboard. Teams quickly see the overall health of a project and can monitor relationships between test, development and other project elements.

Different Types of Software Testing

Acceptance Testing: Formal testing conducted to determine whether or not a system satisfies its acceptance criteria and to enable the customer to determine whether or not to accept the system. It is usually performed by the customer.

Accessibility Testing: Type of testing which determines the usability of a product to the people having disabilities (deaf, blind, mentally disabled etc). The evaluation process is conducted by persons having disabilities.

Active Testing: Type of testing consisting in introducing test data and analyzing the execution results. It is usually conducted by the testing team.

Agile Testing: Software testing practice that follows the principles of the agile manifesto, emphasizing testing from the perspective of customers who will utilize the system. It is usually performed by the QA teams.

Age Testing: Type of testing which evaluates a system's ability to perform in the future. The evaluation process is conducted by testing teams.

Ad-hoc Testing: Testing performed without planning and documentation - the tester tries to 'break' the system by randomly trying the system's functionality. It is performed by the testing team.

Alpha Testing: Type of testing a software product or system conducted at the developer's site. Usually it is performed by the end users.

Assertion Testing: Type of testing consisting in verifying if the conditions confirm the product requirements. It is performed by the testing team.

API Testing: Testing technique similar to Unit Testing in that it targets the code level. Api Testing differs from Unit Testing in that it is typically a QA task and not a developer task.

All-pairs Testing: Combinatorial testing method that tests all possible discrete combinations of input parameters. It is performed by the testing teams.

Automated Testing: Testing technique that uses Automation Testing tools to control the environment set-up, test execution and results reporting. It is performed by a computer and is used inside the testing teams.

Basis Path Testing: A testing mechanism which derives a logical complexity measure of a procedural design and use this as a guide for defining a basic set of execution paths. It is used by testing teams when defining test cases.

Backward Compatibility Testing: Testing method which verifies the behavior of the developed software with older versions of the test environment. It is performed by testing team.

Beta Testing: Final testing before releasing application for commercial purpose. It is typically done by end-users or others.

Benchmark Testing: Testing technique that uses representative sets of programs and data designed to evaluate the performance of computer hardware and software in a given configuration. It is performed by testing teams.

Big Bang Integration Testing: Testing technique which integrates individual program modules only when everything is ready. It is performed by the testing teams.

Binary Portability Testing: Technique that tests an executable application for portability across system platforms and environments, usually for conformation to an ABI specification. It is performed by the testing teams.

Boundary Value Testing: Software testing technique in which tests are designed to include representatives of boundary values. It is performed by the QA testing teams.

Bottom Up Integration Testing: In bottom-up Integration Testing, module at the lowest level are developed first and other modules which go towards the 'main' program are integrated and tested one at a time. It is usually performed by the testing teams.

Branch Testing: Testing technique in which all branches in the program source code are tested at least once. This is done by the developer.

Breadth Testing: A test suite that exercises the full functionality of a product but does not test features in detail. It is performed by testing teams.

Black box Testing: A method of software testing that verifies the functionality of an application without having specific knowledge of the application's code/internal structure. Tests are based on requirements and functionality. It is performed by QA teams.

Code-driven Testing: Testing technique that uses testing frameworks (such as xUnit) that allow the execution of unit tests to determine whether various sections of the code are acting as expected under various circumstances. It is performed by the development teams.

Compatibility Testing: Testing technique that validates how well software performs in a particular hardware/software/operating system/network environment. It is performed by the testing teams.

Comparison Testing: Testing technique which compares the product strengths and weaknesses with previous versions or other similar products. It can be performed by tester, developers, product managers or product owners.

Component Testing: Testing technique similar to unit testing but with a higher level of integration - testing is done in the context of the application instead of just directly testing a specific method. It can be performed by testing or development teams.

Configuration Testing: Testing technique which determines minimal and optimal configuration of hardware and software, and the effect of adding or modifying resources such as memory, disk drives and CPU. Usually it is performed by the Performance Testing engineers.

Condition Coverage Testing: Type of software testing where each condition is executed by making it true and false, in each of the ways at least once. It is typically made by the Automation Testing teams.

Compliance Testing: Type of testing which checks whether the system was developed in accordance with standards, procedures and guidelines. It is usually performed by external companies which offer "Certified OGC Compliant" brand.

Concurrency Testing: Multi-user testing geared towards determining the effects of accessing the same application code, module or database records. It usually done by performance engineers.

Conformance Testing: The process of testing that an implementation conforms to the specification on which it is based. It is usually performed by testing teams.

Context Driven Testing: An Agile Testing technique that advocates continuous and creative evaluation of testing opportunities in light of the potential information revealed and the value of that information to the organization at a specific moment. It is usually performed by Agile testing teams.

Conversion Testing: Testing of programs or procedures used to convert data from existing systems for use in replacement systems. It is usually performed by the QA teams.

Decision Coverage Testing: Type of software testing where each condition/decision is executed by setting it on true/false. It is typically made by the automation testing teams.

Destructive Testing: Type of testing in which the tests are carried out to the specimen's failure, in order to understand a specimen's structural performance or material behavior under different loads. It is usually performed by QA teams.

Dependency Testing: Testing type which examines an application's requirements for pre-existing software, initial states and configuration in order to maintain proper functionality. It is usually performed by testing teams.

Dynamic Testing: Term used in software engineering to describe the testing of the dynamic behavior of code. It is typically performed by testing teams.

Domain Testing: White box testing technique which contains checkings that the program accepts only valid input. It is usually done by software development teams and occasionally by automation testing teams.

Error-Handling Testing: Software testing type which determines the ability of the system to properly process erroneous transactions. It is usually performed by the testing teams.

End-to-end Testing: Similar to system testing, involves testing of a complete application environment in a situation that mimics real-world use, such as interacting with a database, using network communications, or interacting with other hardware, applications, or systems if appropriate. It is performed by QA teams.

Endurance Testing: Type of testing which checks for memory leaks or other problems that may occur with prolonged execution. It is usually performed by performance engineers.

Exploratory Testing: Black box testing technique performed without planning and documentation. It is usually performed by manual testers.

Equivalence Partitioning Testing: Software testing technique that divides the input data of a software unit into partitions of data from which test cases can be derived. it is usually performed by the QA teams.

Fault injection Testing: Element of a comprehensive test strategy that enables the tester to concentrate on the manner in which the application under test is able to handle exceptions. It is performed by QA teams.

Formal verification Testing: The act of proving or disproving the correctness of intended algorithms underlying a system with respect to a certain formal specification or property, using formal methods of mathematics. It is usually performed by QA teams.

Functional Testing: Type of black box testing that bases its test cases on the specifications of the software component under test. It is performed by testing teams.

Fuzz Testing: Software testing technique that provides invalid, unexpected, or random data to the inputs of a program - a special area of mutation testing. Fuzz testing is performed by testing teams.

Gorilla Testing: Software testing technique which focuses on heavily testing of one particular module. It is performed by quality assurance teams, usually when running full testing.

Gray Box Testing: A combination of Black Box and White Box testing methodologies — testing a piece of software against its specification but using some knowledge of its internal workings. It can be performed by either development or testing teams.

Glass box Testing: Similar to white box testing, based on knowledge of the internal logic of an application's code. It is performed by development teams.

GUI software Testing: The process of testing a product that uses a graphical user interface, to ensure it meets its written specifications. This is normally done by the testing teams.

Globalization Testing: Testing method that checks proper functionality of the product with any of the culture/locale settings using every type of international input possible. It is performed by the testing team.

Hybrid Integration Testing: Testing technique which combines top-down and bottom-up integration techniques in order leverage benefits of these kind of testing. It is usually performed by the testing teams.

Integration Testing: The phase in software testing in which individual software modules are combined and tested as a group. It is usually conducted by testing teams.

Interface Testing: Testing conducted to evaluate whether systems or components pass data and control correctly to one another. It is usually performed by both testing and development teams.

Install/uninstall Testing: Quality assurance work that focuses on what customers will need to do to install and set up the new software successfully. It may involve full, partial or upgrades install/ uninstall processes and is typically done by the software testing engineer in conjunction with the configuration manager.

Internationalization Testing: The process which ensures that product's functionality is not broken and all the messages are properly externalized when used in different languages and locale. It is usually performed by the testing teams.

Inter-Systems Testing: Testing technique that focuses on testing the application to ensure that interconnection between application functions correctly. It is usually done by the testing teams.

Keyword-driven Testing: Also known as table-driven testing or action-word testing, is a software testing methodology for automated testing that separates the test creation process into two distinct stages. A Planning Stage and an Implementation Stage. It can be used by either manual or automation testing teams.

Load Testing: Testing technique that puts demand on a system or device and measures its response. It is usually conducted by the performance engineers.

Localization Testing: Part of software testing process focused on adapting a globalized application to a particular culture/locale. It is normally done by the testing teams.

Loop Testing: A white box testing technique that exercises program loops. It is performed by the development teams.

Manual Scripted Testing: Testing method in which the test cases are designed and reviewed by the team before executing it. It is done by Manual Testing teams.

Manual-Support Testing: Testing technique that involves testing of all the functions performed by the people while preparing the data and using these data from automated system. It is conducted by testing teams.

Model-Based Testing: The application of Model based design for designing and executing the necessary artifacts to perform software testing. It is usually performed by testing teams.

Mutation Testing: Method of software testing which involves modifying programs' source code or byte code in small ways in order to test sections of the code that are seldom or never accessed during normal tests execution. It is normally conducted by testers.

Modularity-driven Testing: Software testing technique which requires the creation of small, independent scripts that represent modules, sections, and functions of the application under test. It is usually performed by the testing team.

Non-functional Testing: Testing technique which focuses on testing of a software application for its non-functional requirements. Can be conducted by the performance engineers or by manual testing teams.

Negative Testing: Also known as "test to fail" - testing method where the tests' aim is showing that a component or system does not work. It is performed by manual or automation testers.

Operational Testing: Testing technique conducted to evaluate a system or component in its operational environment. Usually it is performed by testing teams.

Orthogonal array Testing: Systematic, statistical way of testing which can be applied in user interface testing, system testing, Regression Testing, configuration testing and Performance Testing. It is performed by the testing team.

Pair Testing: Software development technique in which two team members work together at one keyboard to test the software application. One does the testing and the other analyzes or reviews the testing. This can be done between one Tester and Developer or Business Analyst or between two testers with both participants taking turns at driving the keyboard.

Passive Testing: Testing technique consisting in monitoring the results of a running system without introducing any special test data. It is performed by the testing team.

Parallel Testing: Testing technique which has the purpose to ensure that a new application which has replaced its older version has been installed and is running correctly. It is conducted by the testing team.

Path Testing: Typical white box testing which has the goal to satisfy coverage criteria for each logical path through the program. It is usually performed by the development team.

Penetration Testing: Testing method which evaluates the security of a computer system or network by simulating an attack from a malicious source. Usually they are conducted by specialized penetration testing companies.

Performance Testing: Functional testing conducted to evaluate the compliance of a system or component with specified performance requirements. It is usually conducted by the performance engineer.

Qualification Testing: Testing against the specifications of the previous release, usually conducted by the developer for the consumer, to demonstrate that the software meets its specified requirements.

Ramp Testing: Type of testing consisting in raising an input signal continuously until the system breaks down. It may be conducted by the testing team or the performance engineer.

Regression Testing: Type of software testing that seeks to uncover software errors after changes to the program (e.g. bug fixes or new functionality) have been made, by retesting the program. It is performed by the testing teams.

Recovery Testing: Testing technique which evaluates how well a system recovers from crashes, hardware failures, or other catastrophic problems. It is performed by the testing teams.

Requirements Testing: Testing technique which validates that the requirements are correct, complete, unambiguous, and logically consistent and allows designing a necessary and sufficient set of test cases from those requirements. It is performed by QA teams.

Security Testing: A process to determine that an information system protects data and maintains functionality as intended. It can be performed by testing teams or by specialized security-testing companies.

Sanity Testing: Testing technique which determines if a new software version is performing well enough to accept it for a major testing effort. It is performed by the testing teams.

Scenario Testing: Testing activity that uses scenarios based on a hypothetical story to help a person think through a complex problem or system for a testing environment. It is performed by the testing teams.

Scalability Testing: Part of the battery of non-functional tests which tests a software application for measuring its capability to scale up - be it the user load supported, the number of transactions, the data volume etc. It is conducted by the performance engineer.

Statement Testing: White box testing which satisfies the criterion that each statement in a program is executed at least once during program testing. It is usually performed by the development team.

Static Testing: A form of software testing where the software isn't actually used it checks mainly for the sanity of the code, algorithm, or document. It is used by the developer who wrote the code.

Stability Testing: Testing technique which attempts to determine if an application will crash. It is usually conducted by the performance engineer.

Smoke Testing: Testing technique which examines all the basic components of a software system to ensure that they work properly. Typically, smoke testing is conducted by the testing team, immediately after a software build is made.

Storage Testing: Testing type that verifies the program under test stores data files in the correct directories and that it reserves sufficient space to prevent unexpected termination resulting from lack of space. It is usually performed by the testing team.

Stress Testing: Testing technique which evaluates a system or component at or beyond the limits of its specified requirements. It is usually conducted by the performance engineer.

Structural Testing: White box testing technique which takes into account the internal structure of a system or component and ensures that each program statement performs its intended function. It is usually performed by the software developers.

System Testing: The process of testing an integrated hardware and software system to verify that the system meets its specified requirements. It is conducted by the testing teams in both development and target environment.

System integration Testing: Testing process that exercises a software system's coexistence with others. It is usually performed by the testing teams.

Top Down Integration Testing: Testing technique that involves starting at the top of a system hierarchy at the user interface and using stubs to test from the top down until the entire system has been implemented. It is conducted by the testing teams.

Thread Testing: A variation of top-down testing technique where the progressive integration of components follows the implementation of subsets of the requirements. It is usually performed by the testing teams.

Upgrade Testing: Testing technique that verifies if assets created with older versions can be used properly and that user's learning is not challenged. It is performed by the testing teams.

Unit Testing: Software verification and validation method in which a programmer tests if individual units of source code are fit for use. It is usually conducted by the development team.

User Interface Testing: Type of testing which is performed to check how user-friendly the application is. It is performed by testing teams.

Usability Testing: Testing technique which verifies the ease with which a user can learn to operate, prepare inputs for, and interpret outputs of a system or component. It is usually performed by end users.

Volume Testing: Testing which confirms that any values that may become large over time (such as accumulated counts, logs, and data files) can be accommodated by the program and will not cause the program to stop working or degrade its operation in any manner. It is usually conducted by the performance engineer.

Vulnerability Testing: Type of testing which regards application security and has the purpose to prevent problems which may affect the application integrity and stability. It can be performed by the internal testing teams or outsourced to specialized companies.

White box Testing: Testing technique based on knowledge of the internal logic of an application's code and includes tests like coverage of code statements, branches, paths, conditions. It is performed by software developers.

Workflow Testing: Scripted end-to-end testing technique which duplicates specific workflows which are expected to be utilized by the end-user. It is usually conducted by testing teams.

Verification and Validation

Verification and Validation is the process of investigating that a software system satisfies specifications and standards and it fulfills the required purpose. Barry Boehm described verification and validation as the following:

- Verification: Are we building the product right?

- Validation: Are we building the right product?

Verification

Verification is the process of checking that software achieves its goal without any bugs. It is the process to ensure whether the product that is developed is right or not. It verifies whether the developed product fulfills the requirements that we have. Verification is Static Testing.

Verification is the process of checking or verifying the credentials, data or information to confirm their credibility and accuracy. In the field of software engineering, software verification is defined as the process of evaluating software product, to ensure that the development phase is being carried out accurately, to build the desired software product.

It is performed during the on-going phase of software development, to ensure the detection of defects and faults in the early stage of the development life cycle and to determine whether it satisfies the requirements of the customer.

Software verification offers answers to our query of "Are we building the software product in a right manner?" However, if the software passes during the verification process, it does not guarantee its validity. It is highly possible that a software product goes well through the verification process, but might fail to achieve the desired requirements.

Activities involved in verification:

- Inspections
- Reviews
- Walkthroughs
- Desk-checking

Features of Software Verification

In the realm of the software industry, software verification plays an integral role in building the product as per the requirements and needs of the customer. Other features of software verification that signify its importance are:

- Performed during the early stages of the software development process to determine whether the software meets the specified requirements.

- Verification denotes precision of the end or final product.

- It conducts software review, walks through, inspection, and evaluates documents, plans, requirements, and specifications.

- It demonstrates the consistency, completeness, and correctness of the software during each stage of the software development life cycle.

- Software verification can be termed as the first stage of the software testing life cycle (STLC).

Types of Verification

Software verifications are of two types, each of which is focused on verifying various aspects of the software and ensuring its high quality. Together, these two verification types ensure that the software conforms to and satisfies specified requirements. The two types of software verification are:

1. Static Verification: Static verification involves inspection of the code before its execution, which ensures that the software meets its specified requirements and specifications.

    *   It is an analysis based approach, usually carried out by just making an analysis of static aspects of the software system, such as the code conventions, software metrics calculation, anti-pattern detection, etc.

    *   It does not involve the operation of the system or component.

    *   Static verification includes both manual as well as automated testing techniques, such as consistency techniques and measurement techniques.

2. Dynamic Verification: It concerns with the working behavior of the software and is being carried out along with the execution of software. Also, known by 'Test phase' dynamic verification executes test data on the software, to assess the behavior of the software.

    *   Unlike static verification, dynamic verification involves execution of the system or its components.

    *   The team selects a group of test cases consisting of tests data, which are then used to find out the output test results.

    *   There are three subtypes of dynamic verification: functional testing, structural testing, and random testing.

Approaches

As stated above, the process of software verification involves reviews, walkthrough, and inspection, which together helps to evaluate the accuracy of the product and ensure its quality. Therefore, defined below are these approaches of software verification:

The process of software verification can be performed through following approaches:

1. Reviews: It is an organized way of examining the documents such as design specifications, requirements specifications, code, etc. by one or more than one person, to explore defects in the software.

2. Walkthroughs: It is, usually an informal way of evaluating the software product, where different teams, whether associated or non-associated with the software development, goes through the software product and have discussion on possible errors and other defects, present in the software.

3. Inspection: It is one of the preferred and most common methods of the static testing. Unlike, walkthroughs, it's a formal way of testing the software, through examination of documents, carried out by the skilled moderator. This method usually, checklist, rules, entry & exist criteria along with preparation and sharing of reports, in order to take corrective & necessary actions.

Advantages of Software Verification

The advantages offered by software verification are numerous. It is among those processes, which makes the process of software development easy and allows the team to create an end product that conforms to the rules and regulations, as well as customer's requirements. Other advantages of this process are:

1. It helps reduce the number of defects found during the later stages of development.

2. Verifying the software in its initial development phase allows the team to get a better understanding of the product.

3. It helps reduce the chances of system failures and crashes.

4. Assists the team in developing a software product that conforms to the specified requirements and design specifications.

Validation

Validation is the process of checking whether the software product is up to the mark or in other words product has high level requirements. It is the process of checking the validation of product i.e. it checks what we are developing is the right product. It is validation of actual and expected product. Validation is the Dynamic Testing.

Activities involved in validation:

1. Black box testing

2. White box testing

3. Unit testing

4. Integration testing

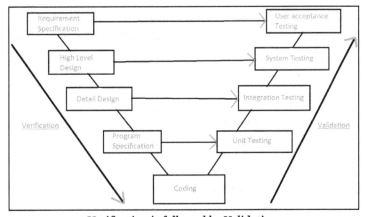

Verification is followed by Validation.

Levels of Software Testing (Validation)

V-Model

The V-model is a type of SDLC model where process executes in a sequential manner in V-shape. It is also known as Verification and Validation model. It is based on the association of a testing phase for each corresponding development stage. Development of each step directly associated with the testing phase. The next phase starts only after completion of the previous phase i.e. for each development activity, there is a testing activity corresponding to it.

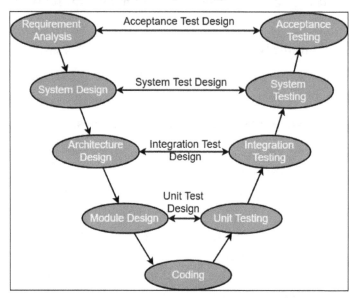

- Verification: It involves static analysis technique done without executing code. It is the process of evaluation of the product development phase to find whether specified requirements meet.

- Validation: It involves dynamic analysis technique (functional, non-functional), testing done by executing code. Validation is the process to evaluate the software after the completion of the development phase to determine whether software meets the customer expectations and requirements.

So V-Model contains Verification phases on one side of the Validation phases on the other side. Verification and Validation phases are joined by coding phase in V-shape. Thus it is called V-Model.

Design Phase

- Requirement Analysis: This phase contains detailed communication with the customer to understand their requirements and expectations. This stage is known as Requirement Gathering.

- System Design: This phase contains the system design and the complete hardware and communication setup for developing product.

- Architectural Design: System design is broken down further into modules taking up different functionalities. The data transfer and communication between the internal modules and with the outside world (other systems) is clearly understood.

- Module Design: In this phase the system breaks down into small modules. The detailed design of modules is specified, also known as Low-Level Design (LLD).

Testing Phases

- Unit Testing: Unit Test Plans are developed during module design phase. These Unit Test Plans are executed to eliminate bugs at code or unit level.

- Integration testing: After completion of unit testing Integration testing is performed. In integration testing, the modules are integrated and the system is tested. Integration testing is performed on the Architecture design phase. This test verifies the communication of modules among themselves.

- System Testing: System testing test the complete application with its functionality, inter dependency, and communication. It tests the functional and non-functional requirements of the developed application.

- User Acceptance Testing (UAT): UAT is performed in a user environment that resembles the production environment. UAT verifies that the delivered system meets user's requirement and system is ready for use in real world.

Industrial Challenge

As the industry has evolved, the technologies have become more complex, increasingly faster, and forever changing, however, there remains a set of basic principles and concepts that are as applicable today as when IT was in its infancy.

- Accurately define and refine user requirements.

- Design and build an application according to the authorized user requirements.

- Validate that the application they had built adhered to the authorized business requirements.

Principles of V-Model

- Large to Small: In V-Model, testing is done in a hierarchical perspective, For example, requirements identified by the project team, create High-Level Design, and Detailed Design phases of the project. As each of these phases is completed the requirements, they are defining become more and more refined and detailed.

- Data/Process Integrity: This principle states that the successful design of any project requires the incorporation and cohesion of both data and processes. Process elements must be identified at each and every requirement.

- Scalability: This principle states that the V-Model concept has the flexibility to accommodate any IT project irrespective of its size, complexity or duration.

- Cross Referencing: Direct correlation between requirements and corresponding testing activity is known as cross-referencing.

- Tangible Documentation: This principle states that every project needs to create a document. This documentation is required and applied by both the project development team and the support team. Documentation is used to maintaining the application once it is available in a production environment.

Why Preferred?

- It is easy to manage due to the rigidity of the model. Each phase of V-Model has specific deliverables and a review process.

- Proactive defect tracking – that is defects are found at early stage.

When to use?

- Where requirements are clearly defined and fixed.

- The V-Model is used when ample technical resources are available with technical expertise.

Advantages

- This is a highly disciplined model and Phases are completed one at a time.

- V-Model is used for small projects where project requirements are clear.

- Simple and easy to understand and use.

- This model focuses on verification and validation activities early in the life cycle thereby enhancing the probability of building an error-free and good quality product.

- It enables project management to track progress accurately.

Disadvantages

- High risk and uncertainty.

- It is not a good for complex and object-oriented projects.

- It is not suitable for projects where requirements are not clear and contains high risk of changing.

- This model does not support iteration of phases.

- It does not easily handle concurrent events.

Unit Testing

UNIT Testing is defined as a type of software testing where individual units/ components of a software are tested.

Unit Testing of software applications is done during the development (coding) of an application. The objective of Unit Testing is to isolate a section of code and verify its correctness. In procedural programming, a unit may be an individual function or procedure. Unit Testing is usually performed by the developer.

In SDLC, STLC, V Model, Unit testing is first level of testing done before integration testing. Unit testing is a WhiteBox testing technique that is usually performed by the developer. Though, in a practical world due to time crunch or reluctance of developers to tests, QA engineers also do unit testing.

Sometimes software developers attempt to save time by doing minimal unit testing. This is a myth because skipping on unit testing leads to higher Defect fixing costs during System Testing, Integration Testing and even Beta Testing after the application is completed. Proper unit testing done during the development stage saves both time and money in the end. Here, are key reasons to perform unit testing.

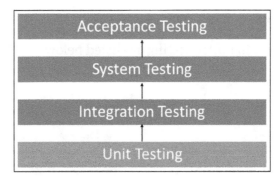

- Unit Tests fix bug early in development cycle and save costs.

- It helps understand the developers the code base and enable them to make changes quickly.

- Good unit tests serve as project documentation.

- Unit tests help with code re-use. Migrate both your code and your tests to your new project. Tweak the code till the tests run again.

How to do Unit Testing

Unit Testing is of two types:

- Manual

- Automated

Unit testing is commonly automated but may still be performed manually. Software Engineering does not favour one over the other but automation is preferred. A manual approach to unit testing may employ a step-by-step instructional document.

Under the automated approach:

- A developer writes a section of code in the application just to test the function. They would later comment out and finally remove the test code when the application is deployed.

- A developer could also isolate the function to test it more rigorously. This is a more thorough unit testing practice that involves copy and paste of code to its own testing environment than its natural environment. Isolating the code helps in revealing unnecessary dependencies between the code being tested and other units or data spaces in the product. These dependencies can then be eliminated.

- A coder generally uses a Unit Test Framework to develop automated test cases. Using an automation framework, the developer codes criteria into the test to verify the correctness of the code. During execution of the test cases, the framework logs failing test cases. Many frameworks will also automatically flag and report, in summary, these failed test cases. Depending on the severity of a failure, the framework may halt subsequent testing.

- The workflow of Unit Testing is 1) Create Test Cases, 2) Review/Rework, 3) Baseline, and 4) Execute Test Cases.

Unit Testing Techniques

Code coverage techniques used in united testing are listed below:

- Statement Coverage

- Decision Coverage

- Branch Coverage

- Condition Coverage

- Finite State Machine Coverage

Unit Testing Example: Mock Objects

Unit testing relies on mock objects being created to test sections of code that are not yet part of a complete application. Mock objects fill in for the missing parts of the program.

For example, you might have a function that needs variables or objects that are not created yet. In unit testing, those will be accounted for in the form of mock objects created solely for the purpose of the unit testing done on that section of code.

Unit Testing Tools

There are several automated tools available to assist with unit testing. We will provide a few examples below:

- Junit: Junit is a free to use testing tool used for Java programming language. It provides assertions to identify test method. This tool test data first and then inserted in the piece of code.

- NUnit: NUnit is widely used unit-testing framework use for all .net languages. It is an open source tool which allows writing scripts manually. It supports data-driven tests which can run in parallel.

- JMockit: JMockit is open source Unit testing tool. It is a code coverage tool with line and path metrics. It allows mocking API with recording and verification syntax. This tool offers Line coverage, Path Coverage, and Data Coverage.

- EMMA: EMMA is an open-source toolkit for analyzing and reporting code written in Java language. Emma support coverage types like method, line, basic block. It is Java-based so it is without external library dependencies and can access the source code.

- PHPUnit: PHPUnit is a unit testing tool for PHP programmer. It takes small portions of code which is called units and tests each of them separately. The tool also allows developers to use pre-define assertion methods to assert that a system behave in a certain manner.

Those are just a few of the available unit testing tools. There are lots more, especially for C languages and Java, but you are sure to find a unit testing tool for your programming needs regardless of the language you use.

Test Driven Development (TDD) and Unit Testing

Unit testing in TDD involves an extensive use of testing frameworks. A unit test framework is used in order to create automated unit tests. Unit testing frameworks are not unique to TDD, but they are essential to it. Below we look at some of what TDD brings to the world of unit testing:

- Tests are written before the code,

- Rely heavily on testing frameworks,

- All classes in the applications are tested,

- Quick and easy integration is made possible.

Unit Testing Myth

Myths by their very nature are false assumptions. These assumptions lead to a vicious cycle as follows:

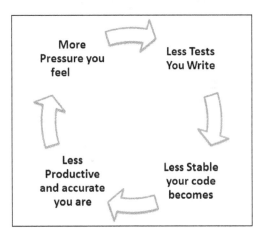

Truth is Unit testing increase the speed of development.

Programmers think that Integration Testing will catch all errors and do not execute the unit test. Once units are integrated, very simple errors which could have very easily found and fixed in unit tested take a very long time to be traced and fixed.

Unit Testing Advantage

- Developers looking to learn what functionality is provided by a unit and how to use it can look at the unit tests to gain a basic understanding of the unit API.

- Unit testing allows the programmer to refactor code at a later date, and make sure the module still works correctly (i.e. Regression testing). The procedure is to write test cases for all functions and methods so that whenever a change causes a fault, it can be quickly identified and fixed.

- Due to the modular nature of the unit testing, we can test parts of the project without waiting for others to be completed.

Unit Testing Disadvantages

- Unit testing can't be expected to catch every error in a program. It is not possible to evaluate all execution paths even in the most trivial programs

- Unit testing by its very nature focuses on a unit of code. Hence it can't catch integration errors or broad system level errors.

Its recommended unit testing be used in conjunction with other testing activities.

Integration Testing

Integration Testing is a level of software testing where individual units are combined and tested as a group. The purpose of this level of testing is to expose faults in the interaction between integrated units. Test drivers and test stubs are used to assist in Integration Testing.

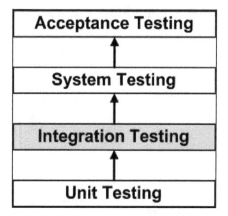

Definition by ISTQB

- Integration testing: Testing performed to expose defects in the interfaces and in the interactions between integrated components or systems. Testing, system integration *testing*.

- Component integration testing: Testing performed to expose defects in the interfaces and interaction between integrated components.

- System integration testing: Testing the integration of systems and packages; testing interfaces to external organizations (e.g. Electronic Data Interchange, Internet).

Analogy

During the process of manufacturing a ballpoint pen, the cap, the body, the tail and clip, the ink cartridge and the ballpoint are produced separately and unit tested separately. When two or more units are ready, they are assembled and Integration Testing is performed. For example, whether the cap fits into the body or not.

Method

Any of Black Box Testing, White Box Testing and Gray Box Testing methods can be used. Normally, the method depends on your definition of 'unit'.

Tasks

- Integration Test Plan

  ○ Prepare

  ○ Review

  ○ Rework

  ○ Baseline

- Integration Test Cases/Scripts

  ○ Prepare

  ○ Review

  ○ Rework

  ○ Baseline

- Integration Test

  ○ Perform

When is Integration Testing performed?

Integration Testing is the second level of testing performed after Unit Testing and before System Testing.

Who performs Integration Testing?

Developers themselves or independent testers perform Integration Testing.

Approaches

- Big Bang is an approach to Integration Testing where all or most of the units are combined together and tested at one go. This approach is taken when the testing team receives the entire software in a bundle. So what is the difference between Big Bang Integration Testing and System Testing? Well, the former tests only the interactions between the units while the latter tests the entire system.

- Top Down is an approach to Integration Testing where top-level units are tested first and lower level units are tested step by step after that. This approach is taken when top-down development approach is followed. Test Stubs are needed to simulate lower level units which may not be available during the initial phases.

- Bottom Up is an approach to Integration Testing where bottom level units are tested first and upper-level units step by step after that. This approach is taken when bottom-up development approach is followed. Test Drivers are needed to simulate higher level units which may not be available during the initial phases.

- Sandwich/Hybrid is an approach to Integration Testing which is a combination of Top Down and Bottom Up approaches.

Tips

- Ensure that you have a proper Detail Design document where interactions between each unit are clearly defined. In fact, you will not be able to perform Integration Testing without this information.

- Ensure that you have a robust Software Configuration Management system in place. Or else, you will have a tough time tracking the right version of each unit, especially if the number of units to be integrated is huge.

- Make sure that each unit is unit tested before you start Integration Testing.

- As far as possible, automate your tests, especially when you use the Top Down or Bottom Up approach, since regression testing is important each time you integrate a unit, and manual regression testing can be inefficient.

System Testing

System testing means testing the system as a whole. All the modules/components are integrated in order to verify if the system works as expected or not.

System testing is done after integration testing. This plays an important role in delivering a high-quality product.

The process of testing of an integrated hardware and software system to verify that the system meets its specified requirements.

Verification: Confirmation by examination and provisions of objective evidence that specified requirements have been fulfilled.

If an application has three modules A, B, and C, then testing done by combining the modules A & B or module B & C or module A& C is known as Integration testing. Integrating all the three modules and testing it as a complete system is termed as System testing.

Approach

It is performed when integration testing is completed.

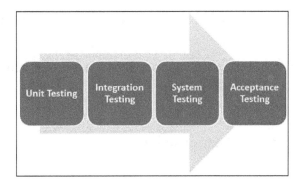

It is mainly a black box type testing. This testing evaluates working of the system from a user point of view, with the help of specification document. It does not require any internal knowledge of system like design or structure of the code.

It contains functional and non-functional areas of application/product.

Focus Criteria

It mainly focuses on following:

- External interfaces
- Multiprogram and complex functionalities
- Security
- Recovery
- Performance
- Operator and user's smooth interaction with system
- Installability
- Documentation
- Usability
- Load / Stress

Why System Testing?

- It is very important to complete a full test cycle and ST is the stage where it is done.
- ST is performed in an environment which is similar to the production environment and hence stakeholders can get a good idea of the user's reaction.
- It helps to minimize after-deployment troubleshooting and support calls.
- In this STLC stage Application Architecture and Business requirements, both are tested.

This testing is very important and it plays a significant role in delivering a quality product to the customer.

Let's see the importance of this testing through the below examples which include our day to day tasks:

- What if an online transaction it fails after confirmation?

- What if an item placed in a cart of an online site does not allow placing an order?

- What if in a Gmail account creating a new label gives an error on clicking the create tab?

- What if the system crashes when a load is increased on the system?

- What if the system crashes and is not able to recover the data as desired?

- What if installing software on the system takes much more time than expected and at the end gives an error?

- What if a website response time increases much more than expected after enhancement?

- What if a website becomes too slow that user is unable to book his/her travel ticket?

Above are just a few examples to show how System testing would affect if not done in a proper manner.

All the above examples are just the result of either system testing not performed or not done properly. All the integrated modules should be tested in order to ensure that the product works as per the requirements.

Is this a White-box or Black-box Testing?

System testing can be considered as a black-box test technique.

Black box testing technique does not require internal knowledge of the code whereas white box technique requires internal knowledge of the code.

While performing System testing functional & non-functional, security, Performance and many other testing types are covered and they are tested using black box technique wherein the input is provided to the system and the output is verified. System internal knowledge is not required.

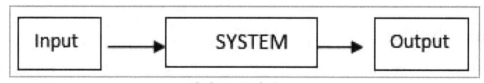

Black Box Technique.

How to Perform System Test?

It is basically a part of software testing and test plan should always contain specific space for this testing. To test the system as a whole, requirements and expectations should be clear and the tester needs to understand the real-time usage of application too. Also, most used third-party tools, version of OSes, flavours and architecture of OSes can affect system's functionality, performance, security, recoverability or installability. Therefore, while testing system a clear picture of how the application is going to be used and what kind of issues it can face in real time can be helpful. In addition to that, a requirements document is as important as understanding the application.

Clear and updated requirements document can save tester from a number of misunderstandings, assumptions and questions.

In short, a pointed and crisp requirement document with latest updates along with an understanding of real-time application usage can make ST more fruitful.

This testing is done in a planned and systematic manner.

Given below are the various steps involved while performing this testing:

- The very first step is to create a Test Plan.

- Create System Test Cases and test scripts.

- Prepare the test data required for this testing.

- Execute the system test cases and script.

- Report the bugs. Re-testing the bugs once fixed.

- Regression testing to verify the impact of the change in the code.

- Repetition of testing cycle till the system is ready to be deployed.

- Sign off from the testing team.

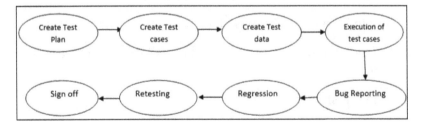

What to Test?

The points stated below are covered in this testing:

- End to end testing which includes verifying the interaction between all the components and along with the external peripherals to ensure if the system works fine in any of the scenarios is covered in this testing.

- It verifies that the input provided to the system provides the expected result.

- It verifies if all the functional & non–functional requirements are tested and if they work as expected or not.

- Ad-hoc and exploratory testing can be performed in this testing after scripted testing has been completed. Exploratory testing and ad-hoc testing helps to unfold the bugs which cannot be found in scripted testing as it gives freedom to the testers to test as their desire is based on their experience and intuition.

Advantages

There are several advantages:

- This testing includes end to end scenarios to test the system.

- This testing is done in the same environment as of the Production environment which helps to understand the user perspective and prevents the issues which can occur when the system goes live.

- If this testing is done in a systematic and proper manner, then it would help in mitigating the post-production issues.

- This testing tests both the application architecture and the business requirement.

Entry/Exit Criteria

Let's take a detailed look at the Entry/Exit criteria for System Test.

Entry Criteria:

- The system should have passed the exit criteria of Integration testing i.e. all the test cases should have been executed and there should be no critical or Priority P1, a P2 bug in an open state.

- Test Plan for this testing should be approved & signed off.

- Test cases/scenarios should be ready to be executed.

- Test scripts should be ready to be executed.

- All the non–functional requirements should be available and test cases for the same should have been created.

- Testing environment should be ready.

Exit Criteria:

- All the test cases should be executed.

- No critical or Priority or security-related bugs should be in an open state.

- If any medium or low priority bugs are in an open state, then it should be implemented with the acceptance of the customer.

- Exit Report should be submitted.

User Acceptance Testing

User Acceptance is defined as a type of testing performed by the Client to certify the system with respect to the requirements that was agreed upon. This testing happens in the final phase of testing before moving the software application to the Market or Production environment.

The main purpose of this testing is to validate the end to end business flow. It does NOT focus on cosmetic errors, Spelling mistakes or System testing. This testing is carried out in a separate testing environment with production like data setup. It is a kind of black box testing where two or more end users will be involved.

Who Performs UAT?

- Client

- End users

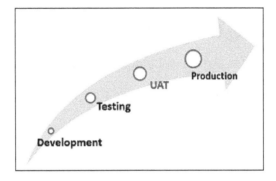

Need of User Acceptance Testing

Once software has undergone Unit, Integration, and System testing the need of Acceptance Testing may seem redundant. But Acceptance Testing is required because:

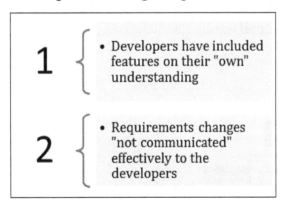

- Developers code software based on requirements document which is their "own" understanding of the requirements and may not actually be what the client needs from the software.

- Requirements changes during the course of the project may not be communicated effectively to the developers.

Acceptance Testing and V-Model

In V-Model, User acceptance testing corresponds to the requirement phase of the Software Development life cycle (SDLC).

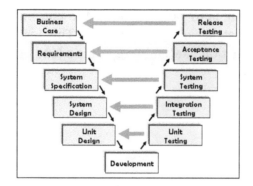

Prerequisites of User Acceptance Testing

Following are the entry criteria for User Acceptance Testing:

- Business Requirements must be available.

- Application Code should be fully developed.

- Unit Testing, Integration Testing & System Testing should be completed.

- No Showstoppers, High, Medium defects in System Integration Test Phase.

- Only Cosmetic error is acceptable before UAT.

- Regression Testing should be completed with no major defects.

- All the reported defects should be fixed and tested before UAT.

- Traceability matrix for all testing should be completed.

- UAT Environment must be ready.

- Sign off mail or communication from System Testing Team that the system is ready for UAT execution.

How to do UAT Testing

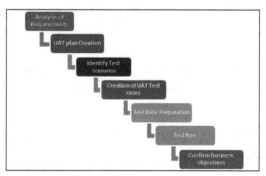

UAT Process

UAT is done by the intended users of the system or software. This type of Software Testing usually happens at the client location which is known as Beta Testing. Once Entry criteria for UAT are satisfied, following are the tasks need to be performed by the testers:

- Analysis of Business Requirements,

- Creation of UAT test plan,

- Identify Test Scenarios,

- Create UAT Test Cases,

- Preparation of Test Data(Production like Data),

- Run the Test cases,

- Record the Results,

- Confirm business objectives.

Step 1: Analysis of Business Requirements

One of the most important activities in the UAT is to identify and develop test scenarios. These test scenarios are derived from the following documents:

- Project Charter,

- Business Use Cases,

- Process Flow Diagrams,

- Business Requirements Document(BRD),

- System Requirements Specification(SRS).

Step 2: Creation of UAT Plan

The UAT test plan outlines the strategy that will be used to verify and ensure an application meets its business requirements. It documents entry and exit criteria for UAT, Test scenarios and test cases approach and timelines of testing.

Step 3: Identify Test Scenarios and Test Cases

Identify the test scenarios with respect to high-level business process and create test cases with clear test steps. Test Cases should sufficiently cover most of the UAT scenarios. Business Use cases are input for creating the test cases.

Step 4: Preparation of Test Data

It is best advised to use live data for UAT. Data should be scrambled for privacy and security reasons. Tester should be familiar with the database flow.

Step 5: Run and Record the Results

Execute test cases and report bugs if any. Re-test bugs once fixed. Test Management tools can be used for execution.

Step 6: Confirm Business Objectives Met

Business Analysts or UAT Testers needs to send a sign off mail after the UAT testing. After sign-off, the product is good to go for production. Deliverables for UAT testing are Test Plan, UAT Scenarios and Test Cases, Test Results and Defect Log.

Exit Criteria for UAT

Before moving into production, following needs to be considered:

- No critical defects open.
- Business process works satisfactorily.
- UAT Sign off meeting with all stakeholders.

Qualities of UAT Testers

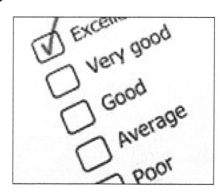

UAT Tester should possess good knowledge of the business. He should be independent and think as an unknown user to the system. Tester should be Analytical and Lateral thinker and combine all sort of data to make the UAT successful.

Tester or Business Analyst or Subject Matter Experts who understand the business requirements or flows can prepare test and data which are realistic to the business.

Best Practices

Following points needs to be considered to make UAT Success:

- Prepare UAT plan early in the project life cycle.
- Prepare Checklist before the UAT starts.
- Conduct Pre-UAT session during System Testing phase itself.
- Set the expectation and define the scope of UAT clearly.
- Test End to End business flow and avoid system tests.
- Test the system or application with real-world scenarios and data.
- Think as an Unknown user to the system.

- Perform Usability Testing.

- Conduct Feedback session and meeting before moving to production.

UAT Tools

There are several tools in the market used for User acceptance testing and some are listed for reference:

- Fitness tool: It is a java tool used as a testing engine. It is easy to create tests and record results in a table. Users of the tool enter the formatted input and tests are created automatically. The tests are then executed and the output is returned back to the user.

- Watir: It is toolkit used to automate browser-based tests during User acceptance testing. Ruby is the programming language used for inter-process communication between ruby and Internet Explorer.

Some Example Guidelines of UAT

- Most of the times in regular software developing scenarios, UAT is carried out in the QA environment. If there is no staging or UAT environment.

- UAT is classified into Beta and Alpha testing but it is not so important when software is developed for a service based industry.

- UAT makes more sense when the customer is involved to a greater extent.

Test Case Design

Software Testing Techniques help you design better test cases. Since exhaustive testing is not possible; Manual Testing Techniques help reduce the number of test cases to be executed while increasing test coverage. They help identify test conditions that are otherwise difficult to recognize.

Boundary Value Analysis (BVA)

Boundary value analysis is based on testing at the boundaries between partitions. It includes maximum, minimum, inside or outside boundaries, typical values and error values.

It is generally seen that a large number of errors occur at the boundaries of the defined input values rather than the center. It is also known as BVA and gives a selection of test cases which exercise bounding values.

This black box testing technique complements equivalence partitioning. This software testing technique base on the principle that, if a system works well for these particular values then it will work perfectly well for all values which comes between the two boundary values.

Guidelines for Boundary Value Analysis

- If an input condition is restricted between values x and y, then the test cases should be designed with values x and y as well as values which are above and below x and y.

- If an input condition is a large number of values, the test case should be developed which need to exercise the minimum and maximum numbers. Here, values above and below the minimum and maximum values are also tested.

- Apply guidelines 1 and 2 to output conditions. It gives an output which reflects the minimum and the maximum values expected. It also tests the below or above values.

Example:

```
Input condition is valid between 1 to 10
Boundary values 0,1,2 and 9,10,11
```

Equivalence Class Partitioning

Equivalent Class Partitioning allows you to divide set of test condition into a partition which should be considered the same. This software testing method divides the input domain of a program into classes of data from which test cases should be designed.

The concept behind this technique is that test case of a representative value of each class is equal to a test of any other value of the same class. It allows you to identify valid as well as invalid equivalence classes.

Example:

Input conditions are valid between

```
1 to 10 and 20 to 30
```

Hence there are three equivalence classes

```
--- to 0 (invalid)
1 to 10 (valid)
11 to 19 (invalid)
20 to 30 (valid)
31 to --- (invalid)
```

You select values from each class, i.e.,

```
-2, 3, 15, 25, 45
```

Decision Table Based Testing

A decision table is also known as to Cause-Effect table. This software testing technique is used for functions which respond to a combination of inputs or events. For example, a submit button should be enabled if the user has entered all required fields.

The first task is to identify functionalities where the output depends on a combination of inputs. If there are large input set of combinations, then divide it into smaller subsets which are helpful for managing a decision table. For every function, you need to create a table and list down all types of combinations of inputs and its respective outputs. This helps to identify a condition that is overlooked by the tester.

Following are steps to create a decision table:

- Enlist the inputs in rows,

- Enter all the rules in the column,

- Fill the table with the different combination of inputs,

- In the last row, note down the output against the input combination.

Example: A submits button in a contact form is enabled only when all the inputs are entered by the end user.

	Rule 1	Rule 2	Rule 3	Rule 4	Rule 5	Rule 6	Rule 7	Rule 8
Input								
Name	F	T	F	T	F	T	F	T
Email	F	F	T	T	F	F	T	T
Massage	F	F	F	F	T	T	T	T
Output								
Submit	F	F	F	F	F	F	F	T

State Transition

In State Transition technique changes in input conditions change the state of the Application Under Test (AUT). This testing technique allows the tester to test the behavior of an AUT. The tester can perform this action by entering various input conditions in a sequence. In State transition technique, the testing team provides positive as well as negative input test values for evaluating the system behavior.

Guideline for State Transition

- State transition should be used when a testing team is testing the application for a limited set of input values.

- The technique should be used when the testing team wants to test sequence of events which happen in the application under test.

Example: In the following example, if the user enters a valid password in any of the first three attempts the user will be able to log in successfully. If the user enters the invalid password in the first or second try, the user will be prompted to re-enter the password. When the user enters password incorrectly 3rd time, the action has taken, and the account will be blocked.

State Transition Diagram

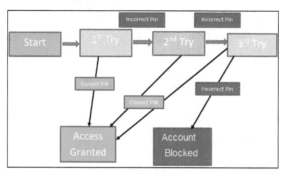

In this diagram when the user gives the correct PIN number, he or she is moved to Access granted state. Following Table is created based on the diagram:

State Transition Table

	Correct PIN	Incorrect PIN
S1) Start	S5	S2
S2) 1st attempt	S5	S3
S3) 2nd attempt	S5	S4
S4) 3rd attempt	S5	S6
S5) Access Granted	-	-
S6) Account blocked	-	-

In the above-given table when the user enters the correct PIN, the state is transitioned to Access granted. And if the user enters an incorrect password, he or she is moved to next state. If he does the same 3rd time, he will reach the account blocked state.

Error Guessing

Error guessing is a software testing technique which is based on guessing the error which can prevail in the code. It is an experience-based technique where the test analyst uses his/her or experience to guess the problematic part of the testing application.

The technique counts a list of possible errors or error-prone situations. Then tester writes a test case to expose those errors. To design test cases based on this software testing technique, the analyst can use the past experiences to identify the conditions.

Guidelines for Error Guessing

- The test should use the previous experience of testing similar applications.
- Understanding of the system under test.
- Knowledge of typical implementation errors.
- Remember previously troubled areas.
- Evaluate Historical data & Test results.

Test Life Cycle

Software Testing Life Cycle refers to a testing process which has specific steps to be executed in a definite sequence to ensure that the quality goals have been met. In STLC process, each activity is carried out in a planned and systematic way. Each phase has different goals and deliverables. Different organizations have different phases in STLC; however the basis remains the same.

Below are the phases of STLC:

- Requirements phase
- Planning Phase
- Analysis phase
- Design Phase
- Implementation Phase
- Execution Phase
- Conclusion Phase
- Closure Phase

Requirement Phase

During this phase of STLC, analyze and study the requirements. Have brain storming sessions with other teams and try to find out whether the requirements are testable or not. This phase helps to identify the scope of the testing. If any feature is not testable, communicate it during this phase so that the mitigation strategy can be planned.

Planning Phase

In practical scenarios, Test planning is the first step of the testing process. In this phase we identify the activities and resources which would help to meet the testing objectives. During planning we also try to identify the metrics, the method of gathering and tracking those metrics.

On what basis the planning is done? Only requirements?

The answer is NO. Requirements do form one of the bases but there are 2 other very important factors which influence test planning. These are:

- Test strategy of the organization.
- Risk analysis / Risk Management and mitigation.

Analysis Phase

This STLC phase defines "WHAT" to be tested. We basically identify the test conditions through the requirements document, product risks and other test basis. The test condition should be traceable back to the requirement. There are various factors which effect the identification of test conditions:

- Levels and depth of testing,
- Complexity of the product,
- Product and project risks,
- Software development life cycle involved,
- Test management,
- Skills and knowledge of the team,
- Availability of the stakeholders.

We should try to write down the test conditions in a detailed way. For example, for an e-commerce web application, you can have a test condition as "User should be able to make a payment". Or you can detail it out by saying "User should be able to make payment through NEFT, debit card and credit card". The most important advantage of writing the detailed test condition is that it increases the test coverage, since the test cases will be written on the basis of the test condition, these details will trigger to write more detailed test cases which will eventually increase the coverage. Also identify the exit criteria of the testing, i.e. determine some conditions when you will stop the testing.

Design Phase

This phase defines "HOW" to test. This phase involves the following tasks:

- Detail the test condition. Break down the test conditions into multiple sub conditions to increase coverage,
- Identify and get the test data,
- Identify and set up the test environment,
- Create the requirement traceability metrics,
- Create the test coverage metrics.

Implementation Phase

The major task in this STLC phase is of creation of the detailed test cases. Prioritize the test cases also identify which test case will become part of the regression suite. Before finalizing the test case, it is important to carry out the review to ensure the correctness of the test cases. Also don't forget to take the sign off of the test cases before actual execution starts. If your project involves automation, identify the candidate test cases for automation and proceed for scripting the test cases. Don't forget to review them.

Execution Phase

As the name suggests, this is the Software Testing Life Cycle phase where the actual execution takes place. But before you start your execution, make sure that your entry criterion is met. Execute the test cases, log defects in case of any discrepancy. Simultaneously fill your traceability metrics to track your progress.

Conclusion Phase

This STLC phase concentrates on the exit criteria and reporting. Depending on your project and stakeholders choice, you can decide on reporting whether you want to send out a daily report of weekly report etc. There are different types of reports (DSR – Daily status report, WSR – Weekly status reports) which you can send, but the important point is, the content of the report changes and depends upon whom you are sending your reports. If Project managers belong to testing background then they are more interested in the technical aspect of the project, so include the technical things in your report (number of test cases passed, failed, defects raised, severity 1 defects etc.). But if you are reporting to upper stakeholders, they might not be interested in the technical things so report them about the risks that have been mitigated through the testing.

Closure Phase

Tasks for the closure activities include the following:

- Check for the completion of the test. Whether all the test cases are executed or mitigated deliberately. Check there are no severity defects opened.

- Do lessons learnt meeting and create lessons learnt document.(Include what went well, where are the scope of improvements and what can be improved).

References

- Software-testing-introduction-importance: guru99.com, Retrieved 19 August, 2019

- Types-of-software-testing: softwaretestinghelp.com, Retrieved 9 April, 2019

- Software-engineering-verification-and-validation: geeksforgeeks.org, Retrieved 2 February, 2019

- Software-verification: professionalqa.com, Retrieved 14 June, 2019

- Unit-testing-guide: guru99.com, Retrieved 8 July, 2019

- System-testing: softwaretestinghelp.com, Retrieved 12 April, 2019

- User-acceptance-testing: guru99.com, Retrieved 22 May, 2019

- Software-testing-techniques: guru99.com, Retrieved 29 January, 2019

- What-is-software-testing-life-cycle-stlc: softwaretestinghelp.com, Retrieved 3 March, 2019

Software Maintenance

The modification of a software product after delivery in order to correct the faults and to improve performance or other attributes is called software maintenance. The topics elaborated in this chapter will help in gaining a better perspective about the software maintenance process as well as the types of software maintenance.

Software Maintenance is the process of modifying a software product after it has been delivered to the customer. The main purpose of software maintenance is to modify and update software application after delivery to correct faults and to improve performance.

Need for Maintenance

Software Maintenance must be performed in order to:

- Correct faults.

- Improve the design.

- Implement enhancements.

- Interface with other systems.

- Accommodate programs so that different hardware, software, system features, and telecommunications facilities can be used.

- Migrate legacy software.

- Retire software.

Categories of Software Maintenance

Maintenance can be divided into the following:

- Corrective maintenance: Corrective maintenance of a software product may be essential either to rectify some bugs observed while the system is in use, or to enhance the performance of the system.

- Adaptive maintenance: This includes modifications and updations when the customers need the product to run on new platforms, on new operating systems, or when they need the product to interface with new hardware and software.

- Perfective maintenance: A software product needs maintenance to support the new features that the users want or to change different types of functionalities of the system according to the customer demands.

- Preventive maintenance: This type of maintenance includes modifications and updations to prevent future problems of the software. It goals to attend problems, which are not significant at this moment but may cause serious issues in future.

Reverse Engineering

Reverse Engineering is processes of extracting knowledge or design information from anything man-made and reproducing it based on extracted information. It is also called back Engineering.

Software Reverse Engineering

Software Reverse Engineering is the process of recovering the design and the requirements specification of a product from an analysis of its code. Reverse Engineering is becoming important, since several existing software products, lack proper documentation, are highly unstructured, or their structure has degraded through a series of maintenance efforts.

Why Reverse Engineering?

- Providing proper system documentatiuon.

- Recovery of lost information.

- Assisting with maintenance.

- Facility of software reuse.

- Discovering unexpected flaws or faults.

Used of Software Reverse Engineering

- Software Reverse Engineering is used in software design; reverse engineering enables the developer or programmer to add new features to the existing software with or without knowing the source code.

- Reverse engineering is also useful in software testing, it helps the testers to study the virus and other malware code.

Maintenance Process

Following are some of the software maintenance processes:

- The implementation process contains software preparation and transition activities, such as the conception and creation of the maintenance plan, the preparation for handling problems identified during development, and the follow-up on product configuration management.

- The problem and modification analysis process, which is executed once the application has become the responsibility of the maintenance group. The maintenance programmer must analyse each request, confirm it (by reproducing the situation) and check its validity, investigate it and propose a solution, document the request and the solution proposal, and finally, obtain all the required authorisations to apply the modifications.

- The process considering the implementation of the modification itself.

- The process acceptance of the modification, by confirming the modified work with the individual who submitted the request in order to make sure the modification provided a solution.

- The migration process (platform migration, e.g., is exceptional, and is not part of daily maintenance tasks. If the software must be ported to another platform without any change in functionality, this process will be used and a maintenance project team is likely to be assigned to this task.

- Finally, the last maintenance process, also an event which does not occur on a daily basis, is the retirement of a piece of software.

Types of Software Maintenance

There are four types of maintenance, namely, corrective, adaptive, perfective, and preventive. Corrective maintenance is concerned with fixing errors that are observed when the software is in use. Adaptive maintenance is concerned with the change in the software that takes place to make the software adaptable to new environment such as to run the software on a new operating system. Perfective maintenance is concerned with the change in the software that occurs while adding new functionalities in the software. Preventive maintenance involves implementing changes to prevent the occurrence of errors. The distribution of types of maintenance by type and by percentage of time consumed.

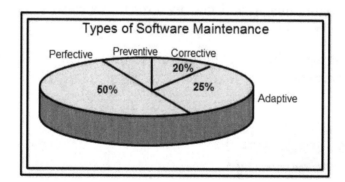

Corrective maintenance deals with the repair of faults or defects found in day-today system functions. A defect can result due to errors in software design, logic and coding. Design errors occur when changes made to the software are incorrect, incomplete, wrongly communicated, or the change request is misunderstood. Logical errors result from invalid tests and conclusions, incorrect implementation of design specifications, faulty logic flow, or incomplete test of data. All these errors, referred to as residual errors, prevent the software from conforming to its agreed specifications. Note that the need for corrective maintenance is usually initiated by bug reports drawn by the users.

In the event of a system failure due to an error, actions are taken to restore the operation of the software system. The approach in corrective maintenance is to locate the original specifications in order to determine what the system was originally designed to do. However, due to pressure from management, the maintenance team sometimes resorts to emergency fixes known as patching. Corrective maintenance accounts for 20% of all the maintenance activities.

Adaptive Maintenance

Adaptive maintenance is the implementation of changes in a part of the system, which has been affected by a change that occurred in some other part of the system. Adaptive maintenance consists of adapting software to changes in the environment such as the hardware or the operating system. The term environment in this context refers to the conditions and the influences which act (from outside) on the system. For example, business rules, work patterns, and government policies have a significant impact on the software system.

For instance, a government policy to use a single 'European currency' will have a significant effect on the software system. An acceptance of this change will require banks in various member countries to make significant changes in their software systems to accommodate this currency. Adaptive maintenance accounts for 25% of all the maintenance activities.

Perfective Maintenance

Perfective maintenance mainly deals with implementing new or changed user requirements. Perfective maintenance involves making functional enhancements to the system in addition to the activities to increase the system's performance even when the changes have not been suggested by faults. This includes enhancing both the function and efficiency of the code and changing the functionalities of the system as per the users' changing needs.

Examples of perfective maintenance include modifying the payroll program to incorporate a new union settlement and adding a new report in the sales analysis system. Perfective maintenance accounts for 50%, that is, the largest of all the maintenance activities.

Preventive Maintenance

Preventive maintenance involves performing activities to prevent the occurrence of errors. It tends to reduce the software complexity thereby improving program understandability and increasing software maintainability. It comprises documentation updating, code optimization, and code restructuring. Documentation updating involves modifying the documents affected by the changes in order to correspond to the present state of the system. Code optimization involves modifying the programs for faster execution or efficient use of storage space. Code restructuring involves transforming the program structure for reducing the complexity in source code and making it easier to understand.

Preventive maintenance is limited to the maintenance organization only and no external requests are acquired for this type of maintenance. Preventive maintenance accounts for only 5% of all the maintenance activities.

Software Maintenance Strategies

Fixed Staff/Variable Schedule Strategy

Figure shows the implementation of the fixed staff/variable schedule strategy. In this implementation, there is a fixed pool of maintenance engineers available to the organization. A maintenance engineer takes a change request off the backlog queue and begins understanding, designing, coding, and unit testing the change. The available staffs' works as many changes as possible through unit test until a "release freeze" is declared by management. The release freeze is scheduled depending on the operational mission needs of the system, but is typically every six months for the systems we observed. Integration test time is scheduled on the operational platform for 30 days after the release freeze. All changes that the engineers declare complete through unit test are then bundled into a release for integration test and formal turnover to the configuration management team. Note there in nothing inherent in the process that precludes code inspections or peer reviews, and some engineers performed them. They were not, however, formalized in the organizations that we observed.

Since the content is determined by the changes the engineers have unit tested up to the release freeze date, and the release schedule is determined by the integration test schedule, this process, should always contain 100% of the unit-tested content and always be delivered on-time. The advantage of this process over the other two is its flexibility in choosing release content and ease with which work is assigned.

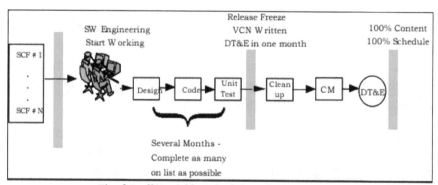

Fixed Staff/Variable Schedule Software Process.

Variable Staff/Fixed Schedule Strategy

Figure depicts the flow of the variable staff/fixed schedule strategy. In this process, there may be a fixed pool of maintenance engineers available, but they are allocated to individual software releases. The product release date is established between the customer and supplier based on a mission need date. Once the date is established and the "high priority" changes are agreed to for the mission, the system analysts prepare a preliminary version content notice (VCN) and a release plan. The preliminary VCN may contain additional changes to the software based on the change request backlog or the schedule. The software engineers begin working on the priority changes while the preliminary VCN and plan are being reviewed by management. If the engineers or managers feel that the VCN is too ambitious or that some changes do not make sense within the context of the version, the content or staffing may be re-negotiated. A final VCN for the release is then issued prior to the completion of all units testing. After unit test the new version is delivered to the configuration management team for integration and operational test prior to formal acceptance by the user.

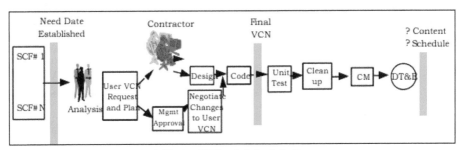

Variable Staff/Fixed Schedule Process.

Since the planned schedule is established between six and eighteen months in advance for this process and some content is negotiable throughout the process, the actual content and delivery date vary with each release. The advantage this process has over the other two is its clearly defined need dates and priority changes. This forces the maintenance team to actively coordinate the release requirements with the user community and focuses the release on achieving the mission goals.

Variable Staff/Variable Schedule Strategy

The variable staff/variable schedule strategy is shown in Figure. In this strategy, there is not fixed staffs of maintenance an engineer, the staff size and skill varies with each release. To determine the release content system users submit a VCN request to the maintenance team. The maintenance team reviews the request and estimates the cost, schedule, and risk associated with the release.

Based on this review, the maintenance team may either add content or negotiate less content with the users. After the content is determined, the maintenance team negotiates a release cost and schedule with a software maintenance contractor to design, code, test, and integrate the release. Milestone reviews are held during the implementation and changes to the plan are made as necessary. The three technical reviews that occur in this process, but are not explicit in the other two processes, are an advantage because the reviews identify issues and help to ensure quality in the release.

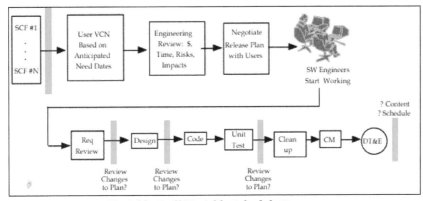

Variable Staff/Variable Schedule Process.

Reverse Engineering

Software Reverse Engineering is a process of recovering the design, requirement specifications and functions of a product from an analysis of its code. It builds a program database and generates information from this.

The purpose of reverse engineering is to facilitate the maintenance work by improving the understandability of a system and to produce the necessary documents for a legacy system.

Reverse Engineering Goals

1. Cope with Complexity.

2. Recover lost information.

3. Detect side effects.

4. Synthesise higher abstraction.

5. Facilitate Reuse.

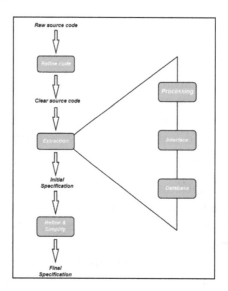

Steps of Software Reverse Engineering

1. Collection Information: This step focuses on collecting all possible information (i.e., source design documents etc.) about the software.

2. Examining the information: The information collected in step-1 as studied so as to get familiar with the system.

3. Extracting the structure: This step concerns with identification of program structure in the form of structure chart where each node corresponds to some routine.

4. Recording the functionality: During this step processing details of each module of the structure, charts are recorded using structured language like decision table, etc.

5. Recording data flow: From the information extracted in step-3 and step-4, set of data flow diagrams are derived to show the flow of data among the processes.

6. Recording control flow: High level control structure of the software is recorded.

7. Review extracted design: Design document extracted is reviewed several times to ensure consistency and correctness. It also ensures that the design represents the program.

8. Generate documentation: Finally, in this step, the complete documentation including SRS, design document, history, overview, etc. are recorded for future use.

References

- Software-engineering-software-maintenance: geeksforgeeks.org, Retrieved 4 August, 2019

- What-is-software-maintenance-explain-maintenance-process: owlgen.com, Retrieved 28 March, 2019

- Types-of-software-maintenance: ecomputernotes.com, Retrieved 8 April, 2019

- Software-engineering-reverse-engineering: geeksforgeeks.org, Retrieved 19 July, 2019

Permissions

Index

www.ingramcontent.com/pod-product-compliance
Lightning Source LLC
Jackson TN
JSHW052211130125
77033JS00004B/230